LANGUAGE AND LITER

Dorothy S. Strickland, Fo[
Celia Genishi and Donna E. Alver[

ADVISORY BOARD: *Richard Allington, Kathryn Au,*
Anne Haas Dyson, Carole Edelsky, Mary Juzwik, Susan Lytle, Django Paris, Timothy Shanahan

continued

For volumes in the NCRLL Collection (edited by JoBeth Allen and Donna E. Alvermann) and the Practitioners Bookshelf Series
(edited by Celia Genishi and Donna E. Alvermann), as well as other titles in this series, please visit www.tcpress.com.

Assessing Writing,
TEACHING WRITERS

Putting the Analytic Writing
Continuum to Work in
Your Classroom

Mary Ann Smith & Sherry Seale Swain

Foreword by Jeffrey D. Wilhelm
Afterword by Linda Friedrich

TEACHERS COLLEGE PRESS

TEACHERS COLLEGE | COLUMBIA UNIVERSITY
NEW YORK AND LONDON

NATIONAL WRITING PROJECT

Published simultaneously by Teachers College Press, 1234 Amsterdam Avenue, New York, NY 10027 and the National Writing Project, 2105 Bancroft Way, Berkeley CA 94720-1042.

Copyright © 2017 by Teachers College, Columbia University

Cover design by Holly Grundon / BHG Graphic Design.

Through its mission, the National Writing Project (NWP) focuses the knowledge, expertise, and leadership of our nation's educators on sustained efforts to help youth become successful writers and learners. NWP works in partnership with local Writing Project sites, located on nearly 200 university and college campuses, to provide high-quality professional development in schools, universities, libraries, museums, and after-school programs. NWP envisions a future where every person is an accomplished writer, engaged learner, and active participant in a digital, interconnected world.

All rights reserved. No part of this publication may be reproduced or transmitted in any form or by any means, electronic or mechanical, including photocopy, or any information storage and retrieval system, without permission from the publisher.

The authors express gratitude for permission to use the following: In Chapter 4, "The Selfie's Screaming Narcissism Masks an Urge to Connect," by Jonathan Freedland, *The Guardian*, 2013. Retrieved from www.theguardian.com/commentisfree/2013/nov/19/selfie-narcissism-oxford-dictionary-word. Copyright Guardian News & Media Ltd 2016.

Library of Congress Cataloging-in-Publication Data

Names: Smith, Mary Ann, 1942–
Title: Assessing writing, teaching writers : putting the analytic writing
    continuum to work in your classroom / Mary Ann Smith, Sherry Seale Swain ;
    Foreword by Jeffery D. Wilhelm ; Afterword by Linda D. Friedrich.
Description: New York, NY : Teachers College Press : National Writing
    Project, 2016. | Series: Language and literacy series | Includes
    bibliographical references and index.
Identifiers: LCCN 2016037362 (print) | LCCN 2016038879 (ebook) | ISBN
    9780807758120 (pbk.) | ISBN 9780807775547 (ebook)
Subjects: LCSH: Composition (Language arts)—Study and teaching.
Classification: LCC LB1576 .S626 2016 (print) | LCC LB1576 (ebook) | DDC
    372.62/3—dc23
LC record available at https://lccn.loc.gov/2016037362

ISBN 978-0-8077-5812-0 (paper)
ISBN 978-0-8077-7554-7 (ebook)

Printed on acid-free paper
Manufactured in the United States of America

24 23 22 21 20 19 18 17   8 7 6 5 4 3 2 1

Contents

Foreword

The most formative and empowering experience of my life as a middle and high school teacher has been to be a National Writing Project (NWP) fellow and teacher-consultant; likewise, the most significant learning and service experience of my university teaching life has been to be, for over 20 years now, a NWP director and thinking partner for teachers K–12. And the reason why is captured in this book. The NWP involves teachers in thinking partnerships about the most significant issues facing teachers and learners, and it's not just about thinking: As you will see, the thinking leads to action and significant doing!

When the NWP asked the Boise State Writing Project (BSWP) Teacher Inquiry Community (TIC) to participate in reviewing, field testing, and researching the use of the Analytic Writing Continuum (AWC) in K–12 literacy and content-area classrooms (with all these acronyms I sound like Robin Williams in *Good Morning, Vietnam*), we leapt at the chance to do work of immense significance to teachers and learners.

Every wide-awake teacher knows that what and how we assess is an opportunity to learn from students how to better teach them, and for students to consolidate learning and to continue moving forward. However, this growth potential is usually unrealized (Hillocks, 1983; 2002), as assessment tends to be merely *of* the achievement. Typically lost is the opportunity of assessment *for* learning (when teachers learn from students what assistance they need next) and assessment *as* learning (when students learn how to name what they have accomplished and how they accomplished it, and what they can do next to move forward to the next challenge). Assessment, we know, directs teaching and, as we also know, it can often get in the way of real learning, leading to formulas that do not reflect expert practice and often undermine it (Hillocks, 1995).

There is a lot to recommend this book, and one central strength is its expression of *the authority of teacher practice*. When my group pursued our teacher research, another central strength stood out. The AWC became a tool *of student inquiry*, a way for learners to inquire into not only their own writing but also the features of good writing, and how good writing is structured and makes certain moves for meaning and effect. It was also a tool *of our teacher inquiry*, giving focus to our professional development work of looking at student writing (and other performances) together, and guiding our subsequent planning and teaching. This tool provided a way to engage as thinking partners across grade levels and content areas, and to develop professionally together.

The AWC's flexibility was another central strength. The AWC allowed us to focus on one or two tools or text features at a time, based on our students' different points of need or the demands of specific situations, assignments, or interests. The AWC also worked for assessing multimedia projects, visual art, and a whole array of other compositions and performances. It was immensely useful in helping us think about focusing instruction, teaching invention, and guiding revision. In other words, the AWC assisted both teachers and writers throughout the whole of the composing processes—from planning to publication.

Perhaps the greatest strength was that the AWC helped us and our students make visible their accomplishments as writers, as well as show what they could do next: to name growth *and* name the way forward. As we used the AWC to give feedback and feedforward, it supported us to provide precise descriptions of what the author had done, the meanings and effects, and the potential for next steps. Strengths and potential were emphasized instead of deficits, as is too often the case with assessment (Hillocks, 1995). The AWC assisted all of us, teachers and students alike, in how to give one another other focused descriptive feedback that traced the process and progress of how meaning and effect was or could be achieved. This means a lot: Nothing is more motivating and empowering than recognizing and naming how one is becoming more competent, and how one can continue to develop in these directions (Smith & Wilhelm, 2003; 2006).

This growth aspect of the AWC is captured by the idea of a continuum. Any composition or performance is a point on a journey—it's just one way station on a trip to somewhere even more complex and rich. In all these ways and many others, the AWC is a tool that powerfully assists learning—of students—and of teachers too. This book will be your thinking partner and travel companion on a journey toward more effective teaching and assessing, and will be a lever for a thinking partnership with colleagues and students. That's what it's done for us.

Jeffrey D. Wilhelm
Distinguished Professor of English Education
Director, Boise State Writing Project

REFERENCES

Hillocks, G. (1983). *Research on written composition.* Champaign-Urbana, IL: NCTE.

Hillocks, G. (1995). *Teaching writing as reflective practice.* New York, NY: Teachers College Press.

Hillocks, G. (2002). *The testing trap.* New York, NY: Teachers College Press.

Smith, M., & Wilhelm, J. (2003). *Reading don't fix no Chevys.* Portsmouth, NH: Heinemann.

Smith, M., & Wihelm, J. (2006). *Going with the flow.* Portsmouth, NH: Heinemann.

Acknowledgments

Thank you to all the members of teacher action research groups in Boise, Idaho; in Upper Peninsula, Michigan; in San Marcos, Texas; and especially to those whose stories we feature in this book:

Paula Diedrich	Debbie Dehoney
Frank Dehoney	Kay Faile
Jerry Hendershot	Jolene Hetherington
Nikki Mathews	Denise Mumm
Connie Van Sickle	

Special thank you to Jeffrey Wilhelm for supporting teacher professionalism, inquiry, and publication.

We also wish to acknowledge the thoughtful contributions of the teachers who participated in surveys, interviews, phone conversations, and email exchanges:

Linda Allsup	Robin Atwood
Mary Baken	Linda Buchanan
Rebekah Caplan	Tracey Freyre
Amanda Gulla	Kevin Lentz
Emily Noble	Kim Patterson
Emma Richardson	Julie Sheerman
Jennifer Smith	Bonnie Stewart

We are grateful to assessment experts who gave us advice and support as we wrote this book:

Linda Friedrich	
Sandra Murphy	Peggy O'Neill

And finally, we are indebted to Paul LeMahieu who, as the former National Writing Project Director of Research and Evaluation, envisioned the Analytic Writing Continuum Assessment System and led its initial development and implementation.

CHAPTER 1

Handwringing Moments in Teaching
What to Do with Student Writing

Grading papers or giving feedback: by any name, it's often a time-consuming, thankless task with no guarantees. At last count, there were some 13 million entries on Google to the search words "grading made easy." No doubt the bulk of these entries will waver from the topic (and we didn't follow the trail for more than a page or two), but the point is this: It takes enormous effort to respond to student work. Whether or not that effort will move students ahead is anyone's guess. So the search is always on for some kind of invention that might make the process more effective and less maddening.

When it comes to writing, giving feedback gets really complicated. Writing is not just one thing. It's seemingly infinite in purposes and audiences, and in the digital age, in its forms. It's developmental. No student enters the ring with the same experiences, opportunities, abilities, or more often these days, with the same native languages. And if that weren't enough to compound the problem, writing is one of those curricular items that enjoys sporadic attention from policymakers. Sometimes they deem it essential, and other times they overlook it entirely (Murphy & Smith, in press).

The result is whiplash—for both teachers and students. One minute, writing is in the backseat. The next minute, it is surging forward. As a result, not every teacher has experience with a writing program. But whether teachers fall in the novice or veteran categories, they still face inevitable and sometimes daunting questions about the writing they've assigned to their students. What to do with the results? How to help students improve? What to look for in a piece of writing and what to do next?

If it were easy to deal with student writing—if, for example, a checklist would suffice—teachers might be searching out the nearest coffee shop where they could order a mocha latte, relax for a moment, and run down the list. But as any teacher will undoubtedly agree, there is no checklist or calculator or smartphone app or any other magic that can account for all the bits that make up a piece of writing.

The truth is that assessing student writing can feel completely random, not to mention stupefying. Randy Koch (2004) confesses that grading college essays counts as a Sisyphean chore:

1

I've nodded off more than once at my dining room table while grading essays, pen in my hand, chin on my chest, and the night outside our patio door swirling with bugs, headlights, and the occasional siren. I've resorted to bribing myself, vowing that once I sit down at the table with a stack of papers, I'll grade three complete essays before I get up again. Then I can have a snack, watch fifteen minutes of the Cowboys football game, or do something physical, like vacuum or take out the trash (both of which are deliciously tempting when I have essays to grade). (para 10)

And if it weren't enough that some teachers have to make deals with themselves to get through a stack of papers, for others, responding and grading brings on a kind of delirium:

When you're two-thirds of the way through 35 essays on why the Supreme Court's decision in the case of *McCulloch v. Maryland* is important for an understanding of the development of American federalism, it takes a strong spirit not to want to poke your eyes out with a steak knife rather than read one more. I have lots of friends who are teachers and professors. Their tweets and Facebook status updates when they're in the midst of grading provide glimpses into minds on the edge of the abyss—and, in some cases, already deranged. (Tierney, 2013, para 5)

So enough is enough. Someone, sometime has to invent a better way. After all, K–12 teachers and their university colleagues have invented solutions to classroom conundrums throughout the ages, including the hall pass, the seating chart, the reading corner, the author's chair, the whole array of stickers and happy notes, and not to be forgotten, the student of the day (week, month, or year). Why not come up with a way to work more effectively with student writing?

THE ANALYTIC WRITING CONTINUUM (AWC)

In this book, we introduce an invention in the writing world that has brought some sanity back to the grading/commenting/responding process. At the start, this invention—a scoring guide with a system for using the guide—addressed an immediate need to assess student writing at a National Writing Project (NWP) scoring event. However, once teachers discovered the Analytic Writing Continuum (AWC), it took off into classrooms for an extended stay where it could benefit student writers.

Our goal now is to put the AWC in the hands of teachers who are interested and ready for something new. We invite our readers to look critically at the AWC as a tool to support student writing achievement in an era when writing is a central means of communication. But because we think teachers should flee from any teaching idea that can't be reinvented for a particular situation with a particular group of students, our invitation comes with this caveat: The AWC is not cast in stone with a single set of directions for how to use it. The best thing to do is to make it your own.

Many teachers are already familiar with scoring guides or rubrics and regularly use them to spell out expectations for an assignment or project. Rubrics also describe what those expectations or criteria look like in varying degrees: from an outstanding paper to one that is not so good. Our rubric serves a similar purpose. It describes varying levels of accomplishment in writing and delineates the attributes of good writing—content, structure, stance, sentence fluency, diction, and conventions—at each level.

Rubrics like the AWC can also do a more important duty. At their best, they can help students identify what it takes to improve their writing. Imagine the breakthroughs in learning when both teachers and students know the meaning of a phrase like "outstanding control and development of ideas and content."

But even with a shared understanding of such attributes, the teaching and learning of writing is a moveable feast with infinite combinations of writers and writing. A distinguishing feature of the AWC is that it has adapted—in both national assessment and in local classroom situations—to a myriad of variations:

- writing of different kinds
- writing in different contexts
- writing at different grade levels
- writing from writers who are at different levels of development with different backgrounds and abilities

In other words, the AWC is a flexible tool that works in multiple capacities—as an assessment tool and as a teaching/learning tool that accommodates diversity of all kinds.

The idea that teaching and assessing writing go hand-in-hand is not new. Typically, however, assessment experts in a large-scale scoring of papers and individual teachers in classrooms live on different planets. For starters, on the lucky occasions when actual student writing is the focus of an assessment, the measurements and outcomes too often fail to have much relevance in a classroom setting. They miss the mark when it comes to daily work with developing writers. One reason is that teachers seldom have a say in how their students' writing is sliced and diced in any kind of outside evaluation. This was not the case with the AWC. Teachers created the framework for its development, and then they created and tested ways to use it in the classroom, giving the AWC credibility among their colleagues. In fact, teachers were central to the entire process.

THE AWC STORY:
A COLLABORATION OF TEACHERS AND RESEARCHERS

When National Writing Project leaders needed a scoring system for a national scoring of student papers, they turned to some great minds in education: researchers, experts in assessment, and teachers. The choice to include teachers makes perfect sense in light of the NWP mission. The National Writing Project is a network of university-based sites that work to improve writing "across disciplines and at all levels, early childhood through university" (NWP, 2010). At each site, NWP teacher consultants—exemplary teachers who participated in NWP institutes and other leadership workshops—provide professional development, conduct classroom research, publish articles, and develop curriculum and other resources. NWP's core belief is that experienced teachers are the key to reform in education, and that writing is a critical skill that must be part of every student's education.

So it is no surprise that writing project teachers were at the table when the NWP convened this group of experts to launch a new assessment system that would account for the diversity of student writing across the country. The task was to set the parameters for what would become a technically sound, rigorous writing assessment. But clearly the teachers were already thinking about classroom uses when they emphasized their classroom-based concerns: "The substance of the writing must outweigh emphasis on conventions." "The focus must be on defining the quality of writing." "We need to be able to accommodate the grade levels and prompts. . . ." "We need to be able to see growth where there is growth" (Swain & LeMahieu, 2012, p. 47–48).

Another job for the teachers and their university counterparts was to study existing rubrics in light of NWP beliefs and values. Would any of the available rubrics be a candidate for the national scoring? Here again, teachers brought their expertise to the conversation about what misfired in many of the possible rubrics:

- the language was negative, leading to a negative view of student writing
- the criteria favored "sophisticated vocabulary" over natural, honest word choices
- the criteria privileged long sentences as somehow superior to other sentence structures
- the rubric in some way invited a pre-imposed or formulaic structure
- conversely, the rubric was vague, with no clear direction about the features of good writing

Ultimately, there was one rubric that stood out from the others. The 6+1 Trait Writing Model, developed by the Northwest Lab, had the advantage of being familiar and credible to many teachers across the country (Swain & LeMahieu, 2012, p. 45). A national panel of assessment experts1 on student writing, along with senior NWP researchers, confirmed the choice of the 6+1 Trait Writing Model as the starting point for the new system. With permission and encouragement from the originators of the 6+1 Trait Writing Model, the panel modified this rubric to create the NWP Analytic Writing Continuum Assessment System.

The AWC debuted in 2005 at the first NWP National Scoring Conference. To date, eight national scoring conferences, with the Analytic Writing Continuum as the centerpiece, have produced student outcome data for numerous local and national studies, spanning grades 3–12. By the end of 2013, 724 teachers from 41 states had served as scorers at one or more national scoring conferences, scoring 48,475 student papers (National Writing Project, 2015).

Standing the test of time is one measure of an assessment system. But in the case of the AWC, which was designed for scoring all types of writing, every year brought another test as new kinds of writing showed up at national scorings, including narrative, informational, and argumentative texts—the big three in the Common Core State Standards. What's more, the papers were not sorted into piles by type or by geographical origin. They were randomly mixed and scorers simply pulled from the stack. At the end of the day, every scoring session produced high reliabilities (see the Appendix). In other words, regardless of location, demographics, writing assignment, or any other mark of diversity, the AWC proved to be a flexible tool.

SPECIAL FEATURES OF THE AWC

Focuses on the Writing

The AWC spotlights the writing, not the writer—one of modifications made to the 6+1 Trait rubric. Why does this shift from writer to writing make a difference? Isn't it helpful to know something about a student when reading his or her writing?

It's certainly true that teachers know their students, their unique voices, their special interests, and sometimes their life stories. However, this invaluable knowledge can cause some mischief when it comes to looking at a piece of writing. Which one of us has not transported our love for a student straight to that student's paper? Our thinking process may go something like this: "This is not Sam's best work, but he's really trying" or "I think I know what Sam wanted to say here." We let our empathy for Sam color the way we view his writing, and on occasion, we even fill in the blanks for him.

Obviously, classroom teachers are not going to have amnesia when it comes to the writers behind the writing. But treating the writing as an artifact, if only for a few minutes, gives many teachers that bit of distance they need to think about what comes next for a student or for a classroom of students. Jennifer Smith, a New York high school teacher who returned to her classroom after the national scoring, shares this perspective: "Now I try to be more objective when I'm reading student writing and not think so much about who is doing the writing. Because I think the more objective I am, the more I can step back, the more I will help my students" (personal communication, June 20, 2008).

Many teachers who have shared their own writing in NWP summer institutes know firsthand what it means when members of their writing response groups attend to the writing rather than fussing over the writer. Responding to the writing itself sounds something like this: "This anecdote worked so well as an example of . . . ." or "I have an idea for how to give the evidence a little more punch . . . maybe a quotation." By concentrating on the writing, peer responders invest in making it better, even making it sing. Working with the writer begins with working on the writing itself.

Provides a Common Language

Ask a veteran writing teacher what she or he looks for in a good piece of writing and you'll probably hear some familiar words, such as "interesting opening," "organization," "supporting ideas," and "strong vocabulary." Naming these attributes sounds easy, but in fact, finding a common language among communities of teachers and students has always seemed nearly impossible. What's more, even teachers in the same school don't necessarily share common experiences or ideas that would bring them into agreement about what these terms mean. For example, some teachers might view organization in an essay as one of four or five structures (for example, chronology, cause-and-effect, comparison-contrast), while others would insist that organization depends on audience, purpose, and content.

The AWC uses familiar terms and explains what they mean. For instance, the term STRUCTURE, as it appears in the AWC, attends to the overall organization of a piece of writing as well as its internal order. At the higher score points of STRUCTURE, descriptors include, among other things, a **purposeful, coherent, and effective arrangement of events, ideas, and/or details,** as well as a **compelling opening and an effective closure that reinforces unity.**

Is it really so important to have a common language about writing among local communities of teachers and students? We know that other disciplines like mathematics come with an accepted set of terms. A *fraction* is a fraction. In writing, however, words such as *thesis, claim, central idea, main message, theme, topic, proposal, problem,* or *proposition* too often get muddled together. What's more, without a common language that specifically describes the attributes of good writing, teachers may spend hours responding to complicated and sometimes convoluted pieces of student writing with little more to go on than phrases such as "unclear," "needs facts," "too much summary," and "good idea." Let's confess: Who has not had to reach for words? One reason teacher scorers in the NWP national scoring sessions gave a thumbs-up to the shared language of the AWC is that it makes writing more teachable and provides a basis for responding to student writing.

Evaluates Writing in a Meaningful Way

One of our favorite stories comes from a former colleague, Keith Caldwell, who was carrying a huge stack of papers from his English classes when he met up with a group of mathematics teachers in the school parking lot. A genial bunch, the math teachers invited Keith to go with them to the local pub. "I wish I could," Keith said, "but I have all these papers to correct." The math teachers looked closely at the stack and then one of them asked, "How do you know there's anything wrong with them?"

Of course, Keith was not planning to go on a hunt for missing commas or other minutiae. But evaluating student writing in a way that informs both teaching and learning has the potential to ruin a teacher's social life and lead to hours of frustration. If there were ever a need for guidance, it's in the realm of responding to or evaluating the wide range of papers that are the bane of the writing teacher's life.

In any assessment, students need to know "what counts as good." A focus on strengths in student writing, describing "what is present" before turning to potential improvements, can help teachers and students map out plans for next steps. For example, in describing the attribute of STRUCTURE, the AWC refers to a compelling order and ideas that are connected by smooth transitions. Here's language a teacher can grab onto when conferencing with her student. "How are your ideas connected? Let's try to put them in a logical order so that you can show the connections."

Uses Analytic Scoring to Its Best Advantage

You don't have to be an assessment guru to grasp the difference between analytic scoring guides and holistic scoring guides. Analytic rubrics describe each feature of the writing separately (content, structure, sentence fluency, and so on). Holistic rubrics put all the features together. There are pros and cons for each one of these approaches. However, analytic guides have an edge when it comes to the classroom, according to Susan M. Brookhart (2013):

> Focusing on the criteria one at a time is better for instruction and better for formative assessment because students can see what aspects of their work need what kind of attention. Focusing on the criteria one at a time is good for any

> summative assessment (grading) that will also be used to make decisions about the future—for example, decisions about how to follow up on a unit or decisions about how to teach something next year. (p. 6)

Now, remember those teachers who did battle with their stacks of papers needing grading? Well, analytic scoring also has something to offer when it comes to the gobs of time it takes to respond to student papers:

> Analytical scoring is not *the* answer, but it is definitely *one* answer to the time problem, because it makes evaluation of student writing not only more consistent but also faster. Teachers who use written scoring guides to assess writing and who teach the scoring guides to their students often find not only that they can score papers rapidly but also that they do not have as much need to write lengthy comments at the end of each paper. The criteria become a kind of shorthand through which student and teacher communicate about writing. (Spandel & Stiggins, 1997, p. 41)

And now for the clincher. If students are to learn the attributes that show up in the analytic scoring guide, most teachers will want to keep the guide around for a good period of time. Indeed, the AWC has the potential for a long shelf life. Here's another reason why:

> General rubrics [like the AWC] use criteria and descriptions of performance that generalize across . . . different tasks . . . students learn general qualities and not isolated, task-specific features. . . . (Brookhart, 2013, p. 9)

Since we are concerned about those millions of people who Google "grading made easy," let's look at the advantages of general or comprehensive rubrics over task-specific rubrics:

- Can be shared with students at the beginning of an assignment, to help them plan and monitor their own work
- Can be used with many different tasks, focusing the students on the knowledge and skills they are developing over time
- Describe student performance in terms that allow for many different paths to success
- Focus the teacher on developing students' learning of skills instead of task completion
- Do not need to be rewritten for every assignment (Brookhart, 2013, p. 9)

A word of caution here. The term *general* is accurate in describing the AWC because of its adaptability across genres. However, the AWC is in no way general when it comes to its very specific descriptors.

Sets Up a Continuum for Growth Across All Types of Writing

We call the AWC a continuum because it represents the reality that every scorer in an assessment or teacher in a classroom has experienced. There are an infinite number of possibilities and ways a student can fashion a piece of writing, which is why scorers will sometimes throw up their hands in frustration and ask, "Is this paper a three or a four?" The same is often true for teachers when they wonder, "Is this paper a B+ or an A-?" The idea of a continuum is that papers fall in a continuous sequence. Adjacent papers on the continuum can have minute differences. In the end, of course, you may still have to put a grade or a score on a paper, but the descriptors in the AWC give meaning to that grade or score.

The six points in the AWC also allow teachers and students to detect growth over time or evaluators to note differences between groups of students. In addition, the AWC reflects the NWP belief that, in reality, writing scores fall along a potentially infinite continuum of score points—even though only six of those points are available as actual scores (Swain & LeMahieu, 2012, p. 50).

Accommodates All Types of Writing and Writing Assignments

As we have noted, the AWC addresses all types of writing. However, one phenomenon that crops up in typical scoring sessions—and also in classrooms—is the discovery of papers that are "off topic." In these cases, we can assume that the writers chose to ignore the prompt or assignment in favor of some better idea. In "The Right to Go 'Off Topic,'" Vicki Spandel (2005) tells the story of a teacher who brings her a well-written paper that has received a low score in a testing situation for having veered from the directions. Rather than addressing *one* endangered species as specified in the prompt, the paper gives readers a bonus with its thoughtful discussion of *two* endangered species. Spandel agrees with the teacher that the paper merits high marks. The problem with this off-topic business, she says, is that "it causes us to assess the simple thing, not the important thing":

> It turns writing assessment into a control issue: *Wander from my topic and you will pay.* We get so hung up on looking at whether writers have precisely addressed a question we cared little about in the first place (the easy thing to assess) that we forget to look at the quality of the writing (the hard thing). . . . If I were teaching math, biology, or driver's education, following directions would matter to me enormously. . . . In writing, though, creativity matters. Spontaneity is a virtue. Originality and perspective define voice. Risk is essential to success. And writers who never think for themselves cannot go anywhere. If I try to control your writing, I will never get the best you have to give—nor do I deserve it. (p. 33)

During scoring sessions using the AWC, teacher scorers read papers without knowing the prompt or assignment. They match up the writing and the scoring guide with student papers we call *anchors*, which serve as models of each score point. Each anchor paper has its own *commentary*—a short description of how this paper exemplifies a 6 score or a 5 score or a 4 score and so on. In other words, there is an abundance of supporting materials in the AWC system, all of it designed to help scorers take the writing itself more seriously than things like the assigned topic.

Maintains Its Flexibility

One problem with the printed word, especially in education, is its immutability. We all know too well the problem with standards or frameworks or curricula that outlive their usefulness (sometimes almost immediately), and still, they reign over the land. This was not the case with the AWC. During the national scoring sessions where the AWC made its debut, teachers served as the table leaders and scorers and, ultimately, as the close-at-hand observers of the way the AWC performed as a scoring guide. They suggested changes where changes were needed. In other words, the AWC did not become a fossil like so many tools we have encountered as teachers. And more important, teachers did not suffer in silence. They took center stage to make the AWC more nimble, more accurate, and more in tune with the papers they were reading from students across the country. Then teachers went on to tailor the AWC to a myriad of classroom purposes.

FROM NATIONAL SCORING TO LOCAL CLASSROOMS

From the outset, the teacher scorers had their eyes on the AWC as something they might take back home for use in their classrooms as a way to focus and organize writing instruction more broadly. During the scoring sessions, they talked endlessly at breakfast, lunch, and dinner about how they might invent ways to teach writing with the AWC as a centerpiece. Was it possible, they asked one another, for the AWC to serve a meaningful purpose outside of a large assessment? In what circumstances might it help all the different writers who could show up in their classrooms? Here are some of the uses they envisioned that became realities:

- As a formative classroom evaluation tool that allows teachers to plan their lessons around what students need to improve in their writing
- As a touchstone for writing conferences during which both teacher and student can share a common language

- As a tool for peer writing groups to make the discussions more productive and, in the process, to teach students how to identify the attributes of good writing
- As a guide for revising papers
- As a pathway for teaching, with signposts like CONTENT and STRUCTURE to focus instruction on what will make a difference in student writing
- As a way to view and discuss mentor texts and other writing models
- As a guide for minilessons and other direct instruction
- As a special tool for students so they can learn about and improve their own writing and so they can make goals for themselves
- As a way to prepare students for a district or state writing exam—a preparation that is more substantial and worthwhile in the long run than the usual one-time-only preparation
- As a model of attributes and descriptors to help teachers craft a customized set of criteria (because a good tool should spawn other good tools)
- As the centerpiece in professional development sessions with colleagues

These uses are ones we will illustrate in the coming pages.

UPCOMING CHAPTERS

We have organized our discussion of the AWC in the following way:

In Chapter 2, we introduce our readers to the Analytic Scoring Continuum. With this introduction, the National Writing Project is releasing the AWC to the field for the first time. Previously, it has been accessible only to those involved in the national scorings. So we concentrate on how the rubric works with student writing, threading our way through all six attributes: CONTENT, STRUCTURE, STANCE, SENTENCE FLUENCY, DICTION, CONVENTIONS.

Then our story moves into classrooms, where five brave teachers decided to use the AWC to teach writing. In Chapter 3, they tell it like it happened, all the moments of enlightenment and despair. In the process, we examine the decisions they made about how to use the AWC and why and how their students at various grade levels responded.

Chapter 4 goes into considerable detail on how to set up shop, using the AWC for teacher research or inquiry. It also includes models and ideas for using the AWC for professional development.

One of our goals is to put the AWC into the hands of our readers with step-by-step directions in Chapter 5 for how to use it in local district or in school scoring sessions. Similarly, Chapter 6 offers a sequenced guide, this time for how to get started using the AWC in the classroom.

Throughout the book we feature examples of student writing, including commentary that picks up the attributes and language of the AWC. In particular, we examine narrative, informational, and argumentative pieces since they are the cornerstones of the Common Core State Standards. We have included references to the Common Core State Standards (CCSS) along the way because teachers deserve to know how any teaching tool plays out in a given policy environment. For those who are already looking beyond the CCSS, we argue that the flexibility of the AWC also makes it adaptable to future changes in policy. Whatever its merits, the AWC cannot claim an afterlife in classrooms unless it spares teachers the age-old dilemma, described by Edward M. White (2007), of feeling "forced to choose between tailoring their teaching to an impromptu test and helping their students learn how to write . . ." (p. iv).

Also throughout this book, we continue to ask ourselves a critical question: Why would teachers take a risk on the AWC—a seemingly complicated tool—and put it to work in their classrooms? In 2008, NWP researchers interviewed teachers to find out how and why they used the AWC with their students. Primary teacher Robin Atwood, now director of the South Mississippi Writing Project, offered this insight:

> . . . It's almost embarrassing to admit because I thought I was such a great writing teacher. I had really focused more on, you know, it's so hard for the young children just to get their thoughts on the paper. And I had focused more on that than purpose and audience. But when you focus more on purpose and audience, then you've given them a reason to put their thoughts on paper and there's not as much of a struggle to do it. Or there's not so much of an avoidance of it. Even those children who don't struggle to do it may not see the point of it without the purpose and the audience.
>
> And it seems that bringing in the craft of it just sort of added a whole new excitement to the writing, to the classroom. Because everybody was always trying to hone their craft now that you can put a name on things. They were trying out, "oh, look the way I opened this" and "look at the way that I used this convention. That means you're supposed to slow down." So there's this conversation about it. There's an excitement about the actual getting down on the paper what was not there before. (personal communication, June 19, 2008)

Finally, we want to recognize that teachers engage in an unimaginable juggling act every day, working to find the "right stuff" and then make it right for every one of their students:

They are teaching students with all their marvelous diversity and with all the languages and life experiences they bring to the classroom. Students cannot be standardized and turned out for distribution like cans of tomatoes. Even the best ideas in the world for teaching writing and learning to write may not always work for every student, especially since students grow in fits and starts and not necessarily at the same rate. (Murphy & Smith, 2015, pp. 8–9)

To the extent that the AWC can work to the benefit of teachers and students, our book will have met its ultimate purpose.

CHAPTER 2

The Attributes of Good Writing

Some time ago, we talked to a group of Missouri teachers who had just participated in a National Writing Project (NWP) national scoring of student papers. Mary Baken, a first-time scorer, observed that "we all have that gut sense about what good writing looks like." However, she noted the value of a tool or set of guidelines that would "help me as a teacher encourage students to more specifically verbalize what is and is not working in their papers." Because Mary was anticipating her fall classes filled with "reluctant freshmen," she felt especially urgent about giving students a common language to help them identify what they do well and build from there (personal communication, June 28, 2013).

Teachers like Baken know well the need for a fundamental understanding of writing itself and for some tools to translate this understanding for students in order to smooth the bumps along the road to teaching writing. In this chapter, we introduce the Analytic Writing Continuum as a lens through which to look at student writing and to decide on next steps for teaching (see Figure 2.1). We will begin with the three kinds of writing named in the Common Core State Standards. Don't let the somewhat detailed discussion of each paper alarm you ("You mean I have to do this?"). This discussion serves the purpose of explaining the AWC to our teacher readers so that you can explain it to your students and use the model writing if you wish. Graham et al. (2013) recommend teaching students to use rubrics so that "students become independent learners in the fullest sense," and so that "the teacher no longer bears sole responsibility for student learning; in particular, he or she does not have to read and review every piece of student writing in detail" (p. 373).

INTRODUCING THE ANALYTIC WRITING CONTINUUM

Notice that the continuum is spread across several book pages. For the national scorings of student papers, the continuum appears on a single 11 x 17 sheet of paper, three attributes on the front side and three on the back. However, presenting the AWC in separate chunks as it is here is very much in keeping with the way teachers use it.

Figure 2.1. Analytic Writing Continuum

CONTENT (Including Quality and Clarity of Ideas and Meaning)		
6. The writing: » Is clear and consistently focused; exceptionally well-shaped and -connected. » Reflects outstanding control and development of ideas and content. » Contains ideas that consistently and fully support and/or enhance the central theme or topic (e.g., well-developed details, reasons, examples, evidence, anecdotes, events, and/or descriptions, etc.). » Includes ideas that are consistently purposeful, specific, and often creative.	**5. The writing:** » Is clear and focused; well-shaped and -connected. » Reflects strong control and development of ideas and content. » Contains ideas that usually support and/or enhance the central theme or topic (e.g., developed details, reasons, examples, evidence, anecdotes, events, and/or descriptions, etc.) » Includes ideas that are usually purposeful, specific, and sometimes creative.	**4. The writing:** » Is generally clear and focused; satisfactorily shaped and connected. » Reflects good control and development of ideas and content. » Contains ideas that satisfactorily support and/or are relevant to the central theme and/or topic. Details, reasons, examples, evidence, anecdotes, events, and/or descriptions, etc., are sometimes developed. » Includes ideas that tend to be predictable but purposeful.
3. The writing: » Has a discernible focus; sometimes shaped and connected. » Reflects limited control and development of ideas and content. » Contains ideas that somewhat support the central theme or topic, but details, reasons, examples, evidence, anecdotes, events, and/or descriptions, etc., are usually poorly developed and are sometimes list-like.	**2. The writing:** » May present several ideas, but no central focus emerges; seldom shaped and connected. » Reflects little control or development of ideas and content. » Contains ideas related to a theme or topic, but they are often confusing or incidental. Details, reasons, examples, evidence, anecdotes, events, and/or descriptions, etc., are gratuitous, list-like, and/or undeveloped.	**1. The writing:** » May announce the topic, but no central focus is present; not at all shaped and connected. » Reflects minimal or no control or development of ideas and content. » Includes few, if any, ideas that are related to the announced topic (e.g., few or no details, reasons, examples, evidence, anecdotes, events, and/or descriptions, etc.).

Figure 2.1. Analytic Writing Continuum (continued)

STRUCTURE

6. The writing:	5. The writing:	4. The writing:
» Presents an organization that enhances the central idea or theme.	» Presents an organization that reinforces the central idea or theme.	» Presents an organization that satisfactorily develops the central idea or theme.
» Presents a compelling order and structure; writing flows smoothly so that organizational patterns are seamless.	» Includes an order and structure that are maintained with a consistent flow of ideas.	» Includes an order and structure that may be predictable.
» Includes a compelling opening and an effective closure that reinforces unity and provides an outstanding sense of resolution.	» Includes a strong and purposeful opening and a closure that reinforces unity and provides a clear sense of resolution.	» Includes a clear opening and a closure that contributes to unity, but the resolution tends to be obvious.
» Includes transitions that are smooth and cohesive.	» Includes transitions that are effective and clearly connect events, ideas, and/or details.	» Includes transitions that work well, but sometimes the connections between the ideas seem forced or predictable.
» Demonstrates a purposeful, coherent, and effective arrangement of events, ideas, and/or details.	» Demonstrates an effective arrangement of ideas, events, and/or details.	» Demonstrates a clear arrangement of events, ideas, and/or details.

3. The writing:	2. The writing:	1. The writing:
» Presents an organization that is minimally adequate for the central idea or theme.	» Presents an organization that is not adequate for the central idea or theme.	» Lacks a sense of direction; organizational problems may obscure the central idea or theme.
» Includes a structure that is formulaic and predictable, or occasionally erratic, inconsistent, or uneven.	» Includes a structure that is a simple listing of loosely connected events, ideas, and/or details.	» Includes ideas, details, or events that are strung together without apparent structure.
» Includes an opening and closing that are mechanical and formulaic, or that may be either too weak to tie the piece together or only vaguely related.	» May include an opening with little direction and a closure that is inappropriate, unconnected, or missing.	» Includes openings and closures that are typically inappropriate or missing.
» Includes few or formulaic transitions, and ideas may pertain to the topic but not to each other.	» May lack transitions and ideas may not pertain to the topic.	» May be too brief to evaluate for structure.
» Demonstrates a mechanical arrangement of events, ideas, and/or details.		

Figure 2.1. Analytic Writing Continuum (continued)

STANCE

6. The writing:
» Consistently and powerfully demonstrates a clear perspective through tone and style.
» Consistently demonstrates distinctive and sophisticated tone or style that adds interest and is appropriate for purpose and audience.
» Exhibits level(s) of formality or informality very well-suited for purpose and audience.

5. The writing:
» Convincingly demonstrates a clear perspective through tone and style.
» Convincingly demonstrates tone or style that adds interest and is appropriate for purpose and audience.
» Exhibits level(s) of formality or informality generally well-suited for purpose and audience.

4. The writing:
» Adequately demonstrate a clear perspective through tone and style.
» Demonstrates tone or style that is adequate for purpose and audience.
» Exhibits formality or informality adequate for purpose and audience.

3. The writing:
» Sporadically or unevenly demonstrates a clear perspective through tone and style.
» Demonstrates uneven tone or style that is minimally adequate for purpose and audience.
» Sometimes exhibits formality or informality inappropriate for purpose and audience.

2. The writing:
» May weakly demonstrate a perspective.
» Shows little discernible tone or style or may show inadequate tone or style.
» Often exhibits formality or informality inappropriate for purpose and audience.

1. The writing:
» Demonstrates little or no apparent evidence of perspective.
» Is flat in tone and lacking in purpose.
» Exhibits formality or informality not appropriate for purpose and audience.

Figure 2.1. Analytic Writing Continuum (continued)

SENTENCE FLUENCY

6. The writing:	5. The writing:	4. The writing:
» Demonstrates a sophisticated rhythm and cadence with very effective phrasing so that each sentence flows easily into the next.	» Usually has rhythm, cadence, and effective phrasing, although occasionally a sentence may not flow smoothly into the next.	» Has some flow and rhythm, although phrasing and connectives may be more mechanical than fluid.
» Includes sentences that vary in structure and length, creating an extremely effective text; fragments, if present, appear deliberately and effectively chosen for stylistic purposes.	» Includes sentences that vary in structure and length and are used effectively; fragments, if present, appear chosen for stylistic purposes.	» Has some variation in sentence structure; fragments, if present, often work for stylistic purposes.
» Includes sentence structures that are consistently logical and clear so that the relationships among ideas are firmly and smoothly established.	» Includes sentence structures that are usually logical and clear so that the relationships among ideas are established.	» Includes sentences that usually establish the relationships among ideas.

3. The writing:	2. The writing:	1. The writing:
» Has little flow or rhythm, and phrasing may be rigid or mechanical.	» Includes some sentences with structural and word placement problems that result in confusion and unnatural phrasing.	» May include connectives that are redundant, overused, or lacking, so that the piece lacks flow.
» Has little variation in sentence structure; fragments, if present, are used indiscriminately.	» Includes a pattern of many simple and monotonous sentences or a pattern of multiple rambling sentences; may include inappropriate fragments.	» Includes choppy, rambling, irregular, or awkward sentences; typically includes several inappropriate fragments.
» Includes sentences that may be illogical or unclear so that the relationships among ideas are only somewhat established.	» Includes sentences that may be unclear or illogical.	» Includes sentences that are unclear and illogical.

Figure 2.1. Analytic Writing Continuum (continued)

DICTION (Language)

6. The writing:	5. The writing:	4. The writing:
» Contains words and expressions that are consistently powerful, vivid, varied, and precise.	» Contains words and expressions that are usually vivid and precise.	» Contains words and expressions that are often clear and precise.
» Contains words that are usually creative and/or sophisticated, but natural and not overdone.	» Contains words that are usually creative and/or sophisticated, but not always natural.	» Contains words that are mostly appropriate and often varied.
» Contains lively verbs and precise nouns and modifiers that add depth and specificity.	» Contains mostly active verbs and words chosen to fit the piece effectively.	» May contain bland verbs or commonplace nouns and inappropriate modifiers.
» May include imagery; when present, it is consistently powerful.	» May include imagery; when present, it is usually strong.	» May include imagery; when present, it is usually simple.
» May include figurative language; when present, it is effective.	» May include figurative language; when present, it is usually effective.	» May include figurative language; when present, it is often predictable.

3. The writing:	2. The writing:	1. The writing:
» Contains words and expressions that are sometimes clear and precise.	» Contains words and expressions that are occasionally clear and precise.	» Contains a limited vocabulary and redundant words and phrases.
» Contains words that are primarily simple and general, yet adequate.	» Contains some vague and/or incorrect words that may be confusing.	» Contains words that are frequently used incorrectly.
» Contains mostly bland verbs or commonplace nouns and inappropriate modifiers.	» Rarely includes imagery or figurative language.	» Contains words that create only general meaning; imagery and figurative language are typically missing.
» May include imagery or figurative language; when present it is simple and generally not effective.		

Figure 2.1. Analytic Writing Continuum (continued)

CONVENTIONS

6. The writing:

» Is almost error-free and demonstrates an outstanding control of age-appropriate standard writing conventions.

» Includes spelling, usage, punctuation, capitalization, and paragraph breaks that are correct to the extent that almost no editing is needed.

» Includes a wide range of age-appropriate conventions intentionally used for stylistic effect.

5. The writing:

» Exhibits few errors and mainly shows effective control of age-appropriate standard writing conventions.

» Includes spelling, usage, punctuation, capitalization, and paragraph breaks that are correct to the extent that minimal editing is needed.

» Includes age-appropriate conventions sometimes used for stylistic effect.

4. The writing:

» Exhibits some errors but demonstrates reasonable control over a limited range of age-appropriate standard writing conventions.

» Includes spelling, usage, internal punctuation, capitalization, and/or paragraph break errors that require minor editing.

» Includes age-appropriate conventions, but they are rarely used for effect.

3. The writing:

» Reflects a limited control of age-appropriate standard writing conventions or reasonable control over a very limited range of conventions.

» Contains errors in spelling, usage, end and internal punctuation, capitalization, and paragraph breaks that require moderate editing.

2. The writing:

» Contains several errors that reflect a struggle with control of basic conventions.

» Contains errors in spelling, usage, end and internal punctuation, capitalization, and paragraph breaks that require extensive editing.

1. The writing:

» Contains many errors of a variety of types scattered throughout the writing: spelling, usage, punctuation, capitalization, and paragraph breaks.

» May be too brief to evaluate conventions.

We hope you notice several aspects of the continuum:

- Content is always first because it is the main course of the writing.
- The AWC starts with a 6 score point (describes superior writing that may have some flaws) and ends with a 1 score point (describes writing that is at a beginning level).
- Each score point provides a range of characteristics and writing abilities rather than a narrow definition of an attribute. This helps us look at writing as a growth process and as something that is teachable.
- The attributes make visible what writing looks like in its many expressions, and they set an expectation for what "quality" means.

THE AWC IN ACTION: ARGUMENTATIVE WRITING

Like any good tool for assessing or teaching writing, the AWC makes more sense when viewed alongside student writing. Caden Reynolds was a ninth grader in Kevin Lentz's English class at a Lexington, Kentucky, high school. Lentz described him as a hard worker, but not necessarily in the area of writing, which was not his favorite. Caden was willing to write—not for the joy of writing—but for his teacher. Lentz observed that when Caden had a choice of what to write or what to revise, he was more enthusiastic about the task. In general, Lentz's students are motivated by choice, which makes an outside assessment situation unappealing to students because they rarely have options when it comes to topics or readings.

In the fall of 2014, Caden participated in a National Writing Project pilot assessment that included other students from around the country. His task on day one of the assessment was to read a packet of four articles and a graph on the subject of whether or not prisoners should be allowed to donate organs for transplant. On day two, Caden had a class period to write an essay arguing his position on prisoner organ donation. Here is his on-demand draft:

> Many people are dying from organ loss. How would you feel if you could potentially save someone's life by donating an organ. I think prisoners should be allowed to donate their organs for a reduced sentence because so many people are on a waiting list for an organ donation, the prisoners could do something good, and we have so many prisoners that said they would donate.
>
> There are dozens of people every day that get added onto a waiting list to get an organ transplant, while there is only a few people actually donated. The number of people on the waiting list has multiplied in the last year while the number of donors has actually

decreased. Currently there are 92,318 more people on the waiting list than people donating. As you can see, we have a shortage of donors. So if prisoners donate organs we would have so much more donors, so many more lives saved.

I think the main reason that we dont have much organ donors is because the donors dont get anything in return. But that would be why prisoners would do it. We need prisoners to do nice things. Maybe this could make a new start for a prisoner. This could help a prisoner out in that way too. Also it lets them get out of prison 60 days earlier. That will help get a bit more donations. It's not like were letting them get out of prison 2 years early, its just 2 months. Also some people say that the prisoners would lie about their health so they could donate an organ but in an article by Beth Pilaino, she says, "All potential living donors must be screened carefully."

In the Maricopa county jail in Arizona, thousands of prisoners signed up to donate. This is just at one jail. Think about the amount of donors we could get if we got this in other prisons/jails across the country. We could shorten the 92,318 margin of people on the waiting list to donors all the way! That would save so many lives. Also, Utah passed a bill that permits prisoners to sign up for organ donation if their death occurs in prison.

Prisoners should be glad to donate their organs. Were not making them, its a choice! But remember, the margin of people on the waiting list to donate is climbing every day, prisoners could donate and do something "good" for a change, and thousands of prisoners already said they would donate in one jail! So think of the lives we could save if this bill is passed.

So let's take a look at this paper, but not in the abstract. The AWC presents six attributes with descriptors to help teachers unlock the mysteries of first drafts and other student efforts. In the following analysis, we have highlighted the AWC language that most closely describes what we see in the paper. It's also the language that will help students learn to analyze and revise drafts like this one.

The good news about CONTENT in this particular paper is that it contains a **generally clear and focused** position with paraphrased **evidence** from the readings ("92,318 more people on the waiting list; In the Maricopa county jail in Arizona . . ."). In the language of the AWC, the **evidence** is **sometimes developed**, which means it is sometimes not developed. Remember, however, we are looking at *what is there*, rather than lamenting *what is not (yet) there*. Regarding STRUCTURE, the writing includes **an organization that satisfactorily develops the central idea.** The confident STANCE includes a conversational **style** that, while informal, **is adequate to purpose and audience.** Although the SENTENCE FLUENCY has **some flow and rhythm**, the sentences have only **some variation,** in spite of an occasional glimpse of sophistication. ("The number of people on the waiting list has multiplied in the last year while the number of donors has actually decreased.") In terms of DICTION, the writing contains words and expressions that are **mostly appropriate and often clear and precise,** even if somewhat limited by bland "to be" verbs. The writing exhibits **reasonable control** of CONVENTIONS, particularly in an on-demand situation.

Now we have a rough analysis of the writing using each of the AWC attributes. Note that we have used only the descriptors because they supply the language for improving a piece of writing such as this one. What happens next is up to the individual teacher. Remember, this is not a large-scale assessment situation where every attribute is under consideration. In contrast, the classroom goal is not to drag this writer through a total makeover addressing every single attribute, but to consider what opportunities for learning this paper presents. What are the best things to teach in this particular writing situation?

With Caden's paper, CONTENT seems to be the first order of business. Is there enough of it? Is it consistently and fully developed? Are the ideas purposeful, specific, and possibly even creative? As we know, the content comes from a packet of reading, and the writing needs to make more of it. For example, one idea from the packet is that prisoners might receive a slightly reduced sentence were they to donate organs, a controversial proposal that has both supporters and naysayers. Caden's essay refers to this proposal, but without framing, context, or reference to the controversy ("Also it lets them get out of prison 60 days earlier. That will help get a bit more donations. It's not like were letting them get out of prison 2 years early . . . "). So the mention of a reward for prisoners simply pops up, unaided by an introduction or development. A first step in taking this writing to a next level is to teach Caden (and no doubt his peers) to take control of ideas like this one in order to give them shape and relevance.

Revising the CONTENT—fleshing it out more fully—will certainly change what happens to the STRUCTURE and organization. Here again is where teacher decision-making really counts. Teachers know how much stamina their students have for revision. It may be that working on content is enough without diving back in to make the paper structurally seamless. Sometimes if teachers want to add in one more attribute to the revision process, that attribute might be related to content but on a different order of magnitude. Caden's writing, for instance, presents a golden opportunity to focus on SENTENCE FLUENCY and, in particular, sentence variety. As it is, the writing depends on a few frequently-used constructions: *there are, this could, that will, this is.* Teaching Caden some alternatives and how to use them makes an immediate, visible difference in the writing, often enhancing content at the same time. What's more, in the best of circumstances, those options for constructing sentences will be available for Caden to use in future writing situations.

With the AWC in hand, teachers and students don't have to go on a hunting expedition to figure out clearly and specifically where a paper is strong and where it might be improved. The point is not that all teachers using the AWC would make the same decisions about Caden's paper, but that they have a tool to help make those decisions.

That said, the universe of writing instruction is hardly short of tools—many of them prescriptive and devoid of context. Let's be clear about where the AWC fits into this universe. The AWC is meaningful *in context*, and, more precisely, in the presence of a piece of writing. It is meaningful when teachers and students are using it to improve their writing. It comes without a script that dictates how and when to use it, in what circumstances, with what kinds of writing. It does not eliminate the teacher. It depends on the teacher.

THE AWC IN ACTION: NARRATIVE WRITING

Tracey Freyre currently teaches long-term English learners, many of whom were born in the United States or came to this country at a very young age but never reached English proficiency. Some of these students read way below grade level, as low as sixth grade. Understandably, a number of them have low motivation and are resistant readers and writers. So Freyre works with them in English support classes, intended to help students catch up with their native-English-speaking peers.

The piece below actually came from an English Language Development (ELD) class Freyre taught a few years ago. In this class, Freyre taught students like eleventh grader Fabiola Prieto, who had been in this country for 2 to 3 years (personal communication, October 3, 2015).

September 28, 2010

The Disagreement

How can I make two decisions between that I love? Why I have to chose, I ask to myself raising my head up looking at the sky sitting in the school yard.

Hey lets go. "Let do a complot against the teacher." said Luis Enrique one of my classmates.

Yes! Answered Alejandro

"But I don't think Fabiola wants to go, she is the spoiled of the teacher. "Replied Vanessa.

The student wanted to make a revolution against the teacher like Mexico did in 1910. It was a big deal. But the worst thing was that I was between them.

The teacher was an English teacher and his nick name was "el teacher." he was like a second father to me, he gave me advice, he knew when I was sad and when I had problems in my house. I loved him.

"Fabiola you have to come with us. We are a united group. We know that the teacher is very nice with you but you have to understand us. If we don't know one word in English he wants us to repeat the word 100 times. IT is not fear." insisted Luis Enrique with a frightened look.

"I will think about it." That was all that I said.

"The teacher is my best teacher, I know that sometimes he yell at me too but he has reason, all the time he just want us to be good students." I was thinking to myself.

"What should I do? Should I go with my classmates? Or stay in the classroom being like the dark dunk." I questioned.

The bell rang. We went to the classroom my classmates made a circle, they were whispering.

"Fabiola we have a plan when the teacher say something bade to us like that I have sh*t in my head, we all going to outside and tell father Jose."

We heard steps. The teacher was coming dressing like a lawyer with a tie and a briefcase. He was sitting on the big chair. He screamed "you guys are my worst group except for a few of you. You guys have Teflon heads." He said that very angry.

The students were standing up one bye one. I was the last one. I looked at the teacher and he looked at me, I can remember his sad look while I was standing up very slowly. It was one of the wrong decisions that I have made.

We went with the principal the father Carlos just ignored us.

"All of you guys have to say sorry to the teacher." he demanded that pointing to us.

I ran back to the classroom. There was el teacher almost crying.

"Teacher, teacher sorry I am sorry."

"I know I know I know." That was all that he said, hugging me.

When I look back on that day I think of how fortunate I was in having el teacher next to me giving me advice. That day I learn that he wanted me to be good, even if he yell me. I miss him a lot. I hopes one day see him again and say thanks to him.

This story captures the tension the narrator faces when she has to choose between her conscience and her peer group. In the language of the AWC, it reflects **good control and development of ideas and content**, largely through dialogue. In fact, the dialogue works effectively in many ways, especially when it comes to STANCE. **A clear perspective** indeed! Even the STRUCTURE impresses with its **clear arrangement of events**, again accomplished through the use of dialogue.

Of course, all is not clear. The DICTION represents some struggle with the language but it also reveals a determination to use **precise words** ("revolution," "united," "advice," "wrong decisions," "fortunate") and **vivid expressions** ("raising my head up looking at the sky," "dressing like a lawyer with a tie and briefcase," "standing up one bye one"). When it comes to CONVENTIONS, we can note the correctness in initial capitals, final punctuation, and a generally good use of quotation marks. Yet the opportunities for teaching are many, and Freyre faces the familiar question, "What next?"

Here's where a GPS like the AWC can do its "recalculating." Rather than viewing the paper as awash in deficits, the AWC points to assets. It's hard to imagine a learning journey that doesn't begin with finding and naming what works before deciding on the next order of business. As Linda Christensen (2003) points out:

> We start by telling them [students] what they're doing right. Too many students are scarred by teachers' pens in the margins yelling, "You're wrong. Wrong again. Ten points off for that comma splice. Where is the past tense?" Language arts teachers become accustomed to looking for errors as if we will be rewarded in some English teacher heaven for finding the most. (p. 7)

Certainly, Freyre expressed first of all how much she admired this piece of writing for its CONTENT, the fact that **the ideas are purposeful** in establishing the narrator's dilemma and **satisfactorily shaped and connected** as the story unfolds. But content is also high on Freyre's list of next steps:

> I might encourage Fabiola to give some background information . . .
> in order to clarify what had led her classmates to propose this idea
> (perhaps more background about the teacher's personality, showing
> both why Fabiola loved him but also why the students didn't like
> him). . . . the writing could use more description (of characters, setting, etc.) in addition to more emphasis on her own internal conflict,
> perhaps showing her thoughts, feelings in ways besides dialogue.
>   In terms of conventions, the writing points out a struggle with
> punctuation when using tags after dialogue, and at times the past
> tense use is inconsistent, but this is pretty par for the course with English learners, and it looks like for the most part, the writing shows
> decent command of the past tense. (personal communication, June
> 27, 2016)

CONVENTIONS are usually somewhere on the list with English learner (EL) writing. And in fact, Olson, Scarcella, and Matuchniak (2015) suggest that in narrative writing, verb tense, in particular, "can be especially tricky since effective writers deliberately use verb tense in dialogues as it is used in oral language, to convey realistic communication that is representative of specific dialects" (p. 87). As an overall recommendation, the authors advise working with verb tense when giving students feedback on drafts: "When helping EL students edit their draft narratives, teachers will find it valuable to teach or review verb tense. Verb tense endings are difficult for students to hear in speech, because they are rarely pronounced clearly and sometimes EL students' classmates do not use endings in informal oral communication" (p. 87).

Certainly, working with verb tense is part of Freyre's repertoire. However, because Freyre focused on the writing at hand, she decided to put CONTENT before CONVENTIONS as the next step with the biggest payoff.

AWC IN ACTION: INFORMATIONAL WRITING

Senior Clint Linebaugh attended high school in a small town in Missouri. A self-proclaimed avoider of writing, he had a change of heart in Julie Sheerman's year-long English class as he grew familiar with the AWC. Clint completed the draft below during class time.

Marceline

Marceline, the hometown of Walt Disney, is special to me in many ways. This town is where I grew up. It's a small town where everyone knows everybody. There are different places that I can see that brings back memories of my childhood; Main Street, Ripley Park, Chester Ray Stadium, even the Uptown Theater.

Main Street USA is the street that runs straight down the middle of Marceline. The parades we have go down this street for everyone to see. There are some people that spend their day cruising up and down this road to see who is out and about. In Disneyland, the main street there is also modeled from Main Street USA, because Walt Disney loved his childhood home: Marceline.

Right by Mainstreet USA is a little area called Ripley Park. The Carnival occupies this area each year around the Fourth of July. The fun rides, good food, and the best friends is what sets the Carnival apart from any other place in Marceline. I can't remember the last time I didn't go to the Carnival at least once. I can still smell the funnel cakes and the big chiefs people make there.

Down the road, the closed Uptown Theater is found. This is where my family would spend some of our Friday nights. We would watch all kinds of movies on that big screen. The smell of popcorn and candy would fill the air.

If we go east about a block or two, lies the one and only Chester Ray Football Stadium. This brings back some memories of watching high school football games in the stands and watching us win the bell back. Others are of me actually playing on that field in middle school.

This little town is just fine for me. This town gave us an awesome history. It helped grow the best imagination could ever have like Mr. Disney himself. In my mind, this is the best place to live—Marceline.

Notice that this writing is **well shaped and connected** by descriptions of local places and attractions that inspire childhood memories. The **words and expressions are often precise,** including proper nouns and references to specific foods and activities. And here's a bonus: It's not always easy in informational writing to provide a **clear perspective** as opposed to a broad array of facts. In contrast, this writing, with its selection of memories and its connections between Marceline and Disneyland, hits the mark.

Once again, however, our old friend CONTENT needs more attention. Simply put, the writing needs more stuff. More details. More examples. More anecdotes. More descriptions. More purposeful, specific ideas. In fact, what is already present in the paper is so enticing that the reader craves more of everything.

The AWC also offers additional teaching options, depending on the endurance of the student and the time available. One immediate and obvious direction is to punch up Clint's paper with more active verbs. Another choice might be to enhance the sights, sounds, and smells with even more powerful imagery.

Students in Sheerman's class know the AWC backwards and forwards. Sheerman spends time teaching students the AWC's terms to provide a common language for discussing their writing and for looking collectively at various writing samples. During biweekly conferences, she invites students to bring a question about their emerging papers using the language from the AWC. Sheerman also prepares a question for the student based on the AWC (personal communication, June 20, 2008). It's this kind of back-and-forth that helps students make revisions in CONTENT and in the other attributes. Using the AWC in this way also sets up the expectation that a draft is a draft. Revisions matter.

Taking advantage of a rubric like the AWC to help students revise their papers has proven results:

> Two meta-analyses 25 years apart (Graham et al., 2011; Hillocks, 1986) support a conclusion that instruction in evaluation criteria with practice making revisions has a positive impact on writing quality. (MacArthur, 2016, p. 283.)

On the following pages, we explore each attribute of the AWC alongside examples of student work. You may want to flip back and forth between the continuum (Figure 2.1) and the writing as we go. For each attribute, we will unpack the language, listen to what teachers have said about the attribute, and see how the attribute shows up in student writing.

DEFINING THE AWC ATTRIBUTES

Content

> The content attribute describes how effectively the writing establishes and maintains a focus, selects and integrates ideas related to content (i.e., information, events, emotions, opinions, and perspectives), and includes evidence, details, reasons, anecdotes, examples, descriptions, and characteristics to support, develop, and/or illustrate ideas.

Teachers who have grappled with the AWC descriptor of content note its depth and breadth. CONTENT includes the big idea of a piece of writing and a range of options for fleshing out that big idea. As Indiana teacher Bonnie Stewart put it after working with the attribute of content in a scoring session: "I think now I'm a little more specific in what I'm asking from the kids. When I tell them about staying focused, I say, 'You can talk about this topic and you can talk about this topic, but how do they fit together? How do you tie the ideas together into one whole piece?'" (personal communication, June 18, 2009).

Writing teachers know that content is one of those abstract terms that cause students' eyes to glaze over. We hear ourselves saying over and over again, "You need to develop your ideas." We might as well be saying, "Don't forget your jacket. It's cold outside." Yeah. Yeah. Yeah. Mississippi primary teacher Linda Allsup describes how she approached content in a more experiential way after working with the AWC. "Like so many of my colleagues, I struggled with getting kids to develop details centered on their chosen topic. Finally, I took them through some freewriting exercises to build some meat onto the things they had already come up with in their prewriting. Then we picked out one or two things to really hone in on. We went back and looked at examples of what other writers have done and then applied it to the students' writing" (personal communication, June 18, 2008).

In both of these instances, teachers talked to their students productively and specifically about aspects of CONTENT—finding and keeping a focus and generating ideas—with the help of precise words.

In his book *The Testing Trap*, George Hillocks Jr. (2002) treats the development of content as a primary endeavor for teachers and students. "The reader needs enough detail to interact with the thinking of the writer," he states (p. 199). Hillocks takes issue with the teaching strategy that focuses on the structure of a piece of writing, i.e., the five-paragraph theme, in order to show students what goes where. Instead, Hillocks recommends an inquiry approach to engage students in "collecting and evaluating evidence, comparing and contrasting cases to develop inferences about the similarities and differences, creating hypothetical examples to clarify ideas, explaining how evidence supports or does not support a claim, imagining situations from perspectives other than one's own . . . " (p. 200). In other words, CONTENT is the first order of business; everything else—for example, structure—is in the service of content.

Professional writers agree. David Brooks, columnist for the *New York Times*, has this to say about where developing content fits into the process of writing: "I tell college students that by the time they sit down at the keyboard to write their essays, they should be at least 80 percent done. That's because 'writing' is mostly gathering and structuring ideas" (Brooks, 2013).

Graham and Harris (2013) also agree. They note there are "scientific intervention studies showing that methods used to help students access or organize topic knowledge *in advance of writing* [emphasis added] improves the quality of what they write . . . " (p. 18). The authors recommend one scientifically based best practice—prewriting—and also inquiry for acquiring writing content (p. 19). Note that the term "inquiry" refers to the idea that students explore a range of evidence and perspectives, accumulating as much available knowledge as they can before sitting down to write.

The CCSS, too, put a premium on developing content through reading, research, and exploring the ideas offered in a variety of media. When students use information from a range of sources, such as remembered movies, television documentaries, video clips, podcasts, reading, research, and personal experience, their writing swells with evidence and authority. Even a small selection of articles can make a difference to the content of a piece. Take a look at what happens when a ninth-grader refers to several sources to reinforce her call for fellow teens to "put down the phone."

> Do you text? Most people do these days. It is an easy way to communicate when you can't talk face to face or on the phone. With texting you can ask multiple people about a social event, and get answers from everyone in minutes. All of these things sound great right? Right, but you may not know about all the negative costs of texting.
>
> Texting can be very distracting and some experts say texting can even be an addiction (Aydt, 2), which is not a good thing when you are driving. Texting and driving at the same time can be very dangerous and has caused many accidents. The National Safety Council estimates that 636,000 car crashes occur each year due to distractions like texting. Through surveys it has been found that 57% of teens text while driving. Taking your eyes off the road for just a few seconds to check a text is worth no life. Many people have found out the hard way about the costs of texting while driving.
>
> Texting can also cause injuries to the thumb or the entire hand. If you text too much you can put strains on tendons in your hand. If this happens you can develop carpal tunnel or other injuries (Fanning; 1).
>
> Sleep can be affected by texting also. Because texting is silent

someone can text for hours late into the night without alerting any one. Some people's sleep can even be interrupted by an "important" text from their friend. (Fanning, 1).

Texting can also endanger school work and grades. It is not uncommon to look around a classroom and see one or two people sneaking texts every minute. If students text in class they can be so immersed in texting and making sure that the teacher doesn't see that they don't pay attention to the lesson. School distractions don't just end in the classroom either. When doing homework or studying, students can text as much as they want. This can result in a student not trying on the homework or not remembering what he or she should.

Texting may have some good aspects but they don't necessarily weigh out the bad. Even though it keeps you in contact with friends and family it can be bad for you. Texting can be a distraction for driving and school work and also cause loss of sleep and injuries. Sometimes it is best to just turn off the phone and put it down.

This piece is packed with **ideas that consistently and fully support or enhance the central theme or topic,** including the percentage of teens who text and drive and the negative effects of texting on sleep and schoolwork. CONTENT is the "big deal" in writing. It's the beef. Building content shows up in the College and Career Readiness Anchor Standard for Writing with phrases like "support claims," "examine and convey complex ideas and information," and "develop real or imagined experiences or events" (Council of Chief State School Officers [CCSSO] & the National Governors Association [NGA], 2010, p. 41).

Structure

The structure attribute describes how effectively the writing establishes logical arrangement, coherence, and unity within the elements of the work and throughout the work as a whole.

The term STRUCTURE includes the overall arrangement of a piece as well as the internal flow of ideas. The descriptors within each score point suggest that STRUCTURE goes beyond counting paragraphs or filling in templates. For example, a superior piece of writing (score point 6) includes an **organization that enhances the central idea, compelling opening, closure that reinforces unity and provides resolution, smooth and cohesive transitions.** In other words, STRUCTURE arises out of a logical arrangement of the parts in order to illuminate the purpose and central idea of the writing.

The word *organization* still functions as a term to designate the way a piece of writing is constructed. But organization is only one aspect of structure. Like the structure of a house, there is the framework, but within that framework are numerous internal supports, passageways, and rooms.

Teachers in the national scoring sessions talked about the "aha" of looking at a piece of writing for its coherence and unity—those internal supports, passageways, and rooms. Mississippi teacher Kim Patterson Roberts reflected on how, as a writing teacher who writes herself, she understands the usefulness of the AWC to a writer. "I went back into that rubric and looked at the language that describes how well the writing moves from one idea to the next. I think that degree of analysis has really helped me be more critical—not critical in a bad way—of my own writing and the writing of students . . . " (personal communication, June 20, 2008).

Professor of English Amanda Gulla turns the AWC into a series of questions when she gauges the effectiveness of structure in a piece of writing: "I look for things like openings and closings. Well, does the writing have an opening? Does it have a closing? Is there a structure that's logical and then within this logic, is it predictable? Is it powerful?" (personal communication, June 20, 2008).

In Julie Sheerman's class, students have their own printed copies of the AWC to use as they move through drafts of their writing. Note in the final draft below how the structure is influenced by the AWC. The writing opens with short, compelling stereotypes of fast-food workers. The details are purposefully arranged. Each paragraph features a different aspect of learning to work at Sonic.

> Smelly clothes. Greasy hair. Low IQ's. These are the reputations given to all fast food restaurant workers. I was all but thrilled to find myself employed at Sonic Drive-In when I turned sixteen, but my options were limited and I was in need of a paycheck.
>
> I heard from a friend that they were hiring, and under pressure from my parents to get a job, I decided to apply. A phone call and a quick interview later made me the newest employee at the restaurant. I was excited at first, especially when I heard that my friend was going to work there too! Then I realized that there was some actual hard, greasy work involved.
>
> First thing, I learned how to make the famous Sonic drinks. There were so many different combinations; I could tell why Sonic prides itself as the "Ultimate Drink Stop." It was impossible to remember everything that was crammed into my mind on the first day. Cherry limeades and watermelon slushes filled my dreams after that first night. I was anxious to learn more, yet scared to have so much responsibility given to me.
>
> After I became a drink-mixing master, I was taught the basics of ice cream. I learned Sundaes, Blasts, Shakes, Hot Fudge Cakes, and Banana Splits. Perhaps the simplest yet the most difficult dessert was

the original ice cream cone. I never imagined how much work it would be to make the frozen treat. My first attempts came out resembling the Leaning Tower of Pisa, or in some cases the falling tower, ending up all over my arm.

The next step in learning to be a carhop was the actual customer service. This part was tricky; it required the dreaded customer interaction, which was somewhat new to me. "Hi, how are you today?" "Do you need any extra ketchup?" and "Would you like your receipt?" became my normal lingo. Counting money was nerve-wracking; if I gave the customer back too much, well, there goes my tips for the night, and if I shorted the customer, it made for some unpleasant complaints. I could feel impatient eyes glaring at me as I counted back change at a snail's pace in attempt to avoid error.

Without a doubt the duty that I was least looking forward to was the order taking machine—aka "the box." It was intimidating; its hundreds of buttons waiting to be pressed in the correct sequence while the customer on the other end of the line rambled off their order at the speed of light. Nevertheless, I had to learn it. At first, someone had to listen in while I attempted to take orders. I had to request that people repeat every other item, and I'm sure that many became annoyed with me.

Eventually, though, I conquered the box. I even thought that many people spoke their orders too slowly. I perfected the art of the ice cream cone, and could count back change in no time at all. I learned the ins and the outs of the place. I knew without a doubt that a big guy in a gold car would arrive right before happy hour ended, park in one of the very end stalls, and order a Route 44 Diet Cherry Coke Zero. Every single day. He never tipped either. I looked forward to the nice guy who ordered a grape slush and an ice cream cone and tipped very well. I picked up on the fact that sixteen year olds were cheap and that old ladies would let you keep their loose change.

All in all, I learned some valuable lessons from my time at Sonic Drive-In. Most importantly, though, I learned that the food industry is not for me! While I am thankful for the things I learned, I am not too sad to move on. Soon I will put my business and customer service skills to use in a new and more formal profession.

This writing provides a model of unity and of how to tie paragraphs together. The idea that ends one paragraph is picked up in some form in the next paragraph:

- " . . . I was in need of a paycheck."
"I heard from my friend that they were hiring . . . "
- "I was going to have to do some actual work . . . "

"First thing, I learned how to make the famous Sonic drinks . . . "
- "I had to request that people repeat every other item, and I'm sure that many became annoyed with me."

"Eventually, though, I conquered the box."

The writing concludes by referring to those "valuable lessons," then resolving to move on and take these new skills in a different direction. Notice that this writing exemplifies all the other attributes as well, but analyzing one attribute at a time allows teachers to hone in and spend some time on each quality of the writing

A final note to this discussion of STRUCTURE as an attribute: The Common Core State Standards for writing make consistent references to structure. According to the CCSS, an informational piece of writing should " . . . convey complex ideas and information clearly and accurately through the effective selection, organization, and analysis of content." An effective narrative, too, requires " . . . well-structured event sequences." Another anchor standard specifies that students "produce clear and coherent writing in which the development, organization, and style are appropriate to task, purpose, and audience" (CCSSO & NGA, 2010, p. 41). Without a doubt, STRUCTURE counts in every kind of writing.

Stance

The stance attribute describes how effectively the writing communicates a perspective through an appropriate level of formality, elements of style, and tone appropriate for the audience and purpose.

In the evolution of the AWC, the STANCE attribute came to replace the idea of voice—an idea that became more and more elusive across widely varying kinds of writing. A commonly held idea of voice is that the personality of the writer should be reflected in the text (Sperling & Appleman, 2011). Instead, NWP leaders envisioned an alternate to the idea of voice. STANCE is the "quality of text that reflects authorial choice and, like other text qualities, can be taught and learned" (Sperling & Appleman, 2011, p. 72).

The shift away from voice and toward STANCE focuses on the writing and the rhetorical and stylistic elements of stance, including textual features, appropriateness to purpose and audience, and strength of perspective (DiPardo, Storms, & Selland, 2011). The concept of STANCE accounts for the fact that writing has to be shaped for particular occasions, some of them formal and some of them not so formal. Rather than setting up an expectation that the writer will adopt a perennially perky voice, the STANCE attribute accommodates writing across the spectrum of purposes and audiences—from enthusiastic to authoritative to questioning.

Indeed, the notion that the writer's personality should show through in any piece of writing has become all too prevalent. Some readers strongly believe that writing should serve as an extension of the writer through which a reader should "hear the writer's voice." Peter Elbow (1999), for one, challenged the idea that a writer should project a single voice from piece to piece:

> It's worth questioning the *mystique* that sometimes surrounds the idea of "finding one's voice"—questioning the assumption that it is necessarily better to have a recognizable, distinctive voice in one's writing. Surely it doesn't make a writer *better* to have a distinctive style. It is just as admirable to achieve Keats's ideal of "negative capability": the ability to be a protean, chameleon-like writer. If we have become so practiced that our skills are automatic and habitual—and thus characteristic—we are probably pretty good . . . as . . . a writer. But a really skilled or professional . . . writer will be able to bring in craft, art, and play so as to deploy different styles at will, and thus not have a recognizable, distinctive voice. (p. 203)

Vicki Spandel (2005) also talks about voice in the context of assessment where students too often encounter banal topics:

> "Why don't students put more voice into their writing?" we ask. Why don't caged animals run more? Writers trying to assume a passion they do not feel for a topic they did not think up should not be expected to kick the voice level above "earnest" . . . Writers who write about what matters to them write with a natural voice. They do not have to put it on like a suit coat. (p. 31)

Clearly, the expectation that writers will always turn up the volume or summon a personality in the name of voice is unrealistic. But no doubt about it. *Voice* is the more familiar term while the concept of *stance* is the new kid on the block. It requires some teaching to help students understand how a writer establishes a perspective by paying attention to tone (formal or informal) and to a style that suits the occasion.

Michigan middle school teacher Paula Diedrich explains how she introduces the idea of STANCE in her classroom: "I focus on the formality/informality section of this attribute first. We talk about getting dressed for the prom versus going out with your friends 4-wheeling. We dress differently for both occasions. We also don't typically wear a ragged baseball hat with a tuxedo" (Diedrich, 2010).

STANCE may sound elusive in the abstract, but when it shows up in a piece of writing, it sometimes jumps from the page. Take a look at the excerpt below, written by a ninth grader as part of an on-demand response to a set of readings about Title IX. The prompt asked students to write an article for a local newspaper about equal opportunities for girls.

Everyone is supposed to be equal, right? Well Title IX tries to ensure that girls get an equal shot at sports. Many schools don't have girls' teams for football, basketball, or wrestling, but Title IX fixes that. Title IX is some very helpful legislation because it makes education equal, helps girls get better grades, and helps girls get on a level field with guys.

Title IX addresses many issues in education, not just sports. Like Obama said in . . . *Entitled to a Fair Shot*, "Title IX isn't just about sports. From addressing inequality in math and science education to averting sexual assault on campus to fully funding athletic programs, Title IX ensures equality . . ." This means that Title IX tries to make education as equal for everyone as possible, in every area as possible. Not just sports. Title IX's main goal is to end all gender discrimination that occurs in education programs that receive federal funding. Title IX tries to make equality a reality. . .

. . . "Don't you agree that everyone needs a fair shot? You would surely want to play your favorite sport in school too. Not just watch everyone else play."

This writing provides a good example of STANCE. It establishes a tone of "friendly authority" that is **appropriate for purpose and audience,** and it demonstrates awareness of a general audience through its opening rhetorical question and the way it defines Title IX: "Everyone is supposed to be equal, right? Well, Title IX tries to ensure that girls get an equal shot at sports." It emphasizes the power of Title IX by listing some gender inequities, followed by "Well Title IX fixes that." Clearly, the writing is in favor of Title IX as a way to address injustices. No one has to hunt around for a **clear perspective.**

What's more, **style** plays a big part in conveying the perspective. Notice the stylistic word repetition: "This means that Title IX tries to make education as equal for everyone as possible, in every area as possible." And there's no denying that the writing attends to purpose and audience with its direct address to the reader: "Don't you agree that everyone needs a fair shot? You would surely want to play your favorite sport in school too. Not just watch everyone else play."

STANCE as an attribute of good writing translates well when it comes to the Common Core State Standards. Most certainly, the CCSS emphasize appropriateness "to task, purpose, and audience" (CCSSO & NGA, p. 41) and the need to "establish and maintain a formal style" (p. 42). The AWC equivalent is that "writing exhibits levels of formality or informality very well suited for purpose and audience" and that "the writing consistently and powerfully demonstrates a clear perspective through tone and style."

Sentence Fluency

> The sentence fluency attribute describes how effectively the sentences are crafted to serve the intent of the writing, in terms of rhetorical purpose, rhythm, and flow.

As an attribute of good writing, sentences are not frivolous creatures headed for extinction, although admittedly they often look like they are on their last gasp on some social media. Think again. The important work of sentences is to carry the reader along a coherent path to increasing understanding of an idea. Sentences need to flow together to accomplish this task. That flow is accomplished through rhythm, logic, and a skillful mix of sentence forms and lengths. To illustrate, we excerpted two paragraphs from two different seventh-grade papers:

> The umpires pause the game and my coach lets my mother in the softball cage. The cage of urine and broken dreams. Get me out. I have never felt so much like a child. My mother helps me stand up and I casually scoot sand over the wet spot in the dirt. I finally get to leave this evil field, leaving only my dignity and a wet spot in the batter's box. (Swain, Graves, & Morse, 2015, p. 34)

This short bit of writing establishes **relationships among ideas** through sentence variety and sequencing. The opening sentence sets the scene and introduces the characters. The next dramatic **fragment, effectively chosen for stylistic purposes,** identifies more specifically the sad situation. The paragraph features **sentences that vary in structure and length,** ending with a cumulative sentence that pulls the events together.

The idea that sentences pull so much weight in tying together ideas is also illustrated in this paragraph:

> I know that everyone can visualize me with computers, but my classmates seem to have a problem visualizing me fishing. Yes, that's right, one of my other most favorite activities I enjoy is fishing. I have been fishing in almost every lake in Northeast Mississippi. It is very thrilling to be out in the middle of a lake, reeling in a whopping five pound catfish. (Swain, Graves & Morse, 2010, p. 85)

It's not hard to fall in love with this description of a kid who is more than a one-dimensional computer person. And who knew? What makes each **sentence flow** easily into the next are relatively simple devices: the initial repetition of "visualize" and "visualizing"; the repetition of the word "fishing" as it is woven into almost every sentence; and the variety in sentence length and complexity, including the last cumulative sentence that brings home the joy of fishing: "It is very thrilling to be out in the middle of the lake, reeling in a whopping five pound catfish."

As an attribute of good writing, SENTENCE FLUENCY is often recognizable to the eye, for example, just in the assortment of sentences. But imagine now how sentence fluency affects the ear. The following reflection made its debut on *Rural Voices Radio* in Mississippi (Hultman, 2015):

Baby Blue Shack

Along the road to my old home in Pontotoc, I'd see a baby blue shack, its paint peeling in strips down the sides. Out in front was a small garden, a cluster of tomato vines tumbling down steel rods, half-hidden in clumps of tall weeds.

Every morning and afternoon, on my way to and back from school, I passed by that baby blue shack, sandwiched between my apartment complex and a run-down barn. An old man worked in the garden, hunching over his tomato vines, disappearing and reforming in the light green waves of wild grass.

One day, I saw him on my way to school, biting into a full, orangey-red tomato. On my way back, he wasn't there. I never saw him again.

The last time I saw that shack, tomato vines and weeds still stood, shuffling gently in the soft sun. A "For Sale" sign was planted firmly among them. I thought, "When I have to go, a bright patch of weeds and tomatoes wouldn't be such a bad thing to leave behind."

Note in this excerpt **the sophisticated rhythm and cadence, the sentences that vary in length,** and **the flow** from sentence to sentence that moves the reader smoothly from one idea to the next. The long cumulative sentences contrast with the shorter, punchier sentences like "I never saw him again," which turn the piece from simple description to contemplation. Clearly these juxtapositions did not happen by chance. Mississippi teacher Emma Richardson has spent considerable time teaching students how to make sentences flow together for rhetorical effect.

In most writing, sentences are the workhorses. They do the job of maintaining consistency in style and tone throughout the piece. They carry the language that expresses ideas precisely. They are the vehicles for phrases or clauses. The AWC descriptions of SENTENCE FLUENCY can help teachers encourage students to use their sentences more effectively to say what they want to say.

Diction

> The diction attribute describes the precision and appropriateness of
> the words and expressions for the writing task and how effectively they
> create imagery, provide mental pictures, or convey feelings and ideas.

Just when we have finished making the case for sentences, we are now about
to proclaim that it's all about words. Who hasn't rejoiced over baby's first
words or listened intently as young children play with sounds and words,
trying them out and moving them around in new configurations? In *Language and Learning*, James Britton (1972) observes the approximations, the
hits and misses children make on their way to oral language proficiency. The
young child not only imitates words but "people's methods of going about
saying things," for example, the approximation of the four-year-old who
says to her mother, "We better cross here, bettern't we?" (pp. 42–43).

It's right up a teacher's alley to promote imitating and experimenting
with language for both speaking and writing, for example, by using mentor
texts or encouraging wordplay. It's also no surprise that students, as part
of learning, sometimes overdo a good thing, piling on adjective after adjective, for example, *the young, sweaty, laughing boys wearing blue, red, and
green T-shirts* . . . . Similarly, as students learn more about language, they
occasionally reach for an important-sounding but ill-fitting word such as
plethora of vegetables. The point is that students learn about DICTION by
trial and error, ramping up the number or length of words on their way to
understanding that the power of language use lies in its appropriateness and
precision.

The following piece comes from a sixth grader who wrote it during a
summer writing camp.

Tranquility

Tranquility is not a thing, but a special place. This place may be
where nothing matters or everything matters. Tranquility can be
silent, or corrupted with noise. My sense of tranquility is centered
with the noises of nature.

I am high above the ground, perched on a branch of the mag-
nolia. I contemplate everything that happened today. I am joined in
my reverie by a friend. We know what we must do; we climb higher
and higher. We stop because the branches become thinner and thinner. We sit back and enjoy the sunset. Soon fireflies fill the air. We are
not afraid of the darkness; we know this tree too well. We know the
curves in the branches, the way they bend, the way they greet our bare
feet with their smooth bark. In the trees, I feel free, though I am con-

nected to a branch. I am free in the sky. A warm breeze connects with my face, bringing warmth to my body.

I wish we could stay up here, perched on a branch, taking in the sounds of the darkness, a dog barking, crickets chirping, the leaves rustling. . . . (Swain, Graves, & Morse, 2015, p. 65)

Certainly, the words and expressions in this excerpt are **powerful, vivid, varied, and precise.** At the same time, they are **natural and not overdone,** for example, "nothing matters or everything matters," "we climb higher and higher," "the branches become thinner and thinner." Where there is **figurative language,** it is **effective:** "We know the curves in the branches, the way they bend, the way they greet our bare feet with their smooth bark." The very last sentence contains **lively verbs and modifiers:** "I wish we could stay up here, perched on a branch, taking in the sounds of the darkness, a dog barking, crickets chirping, the leaves rustling. . . . "

The wonderful thing about teaching DICTION —whether in a summer camp or in a classroom—is that the results are so quickly visible to students. They can see instant improvement in their writing. In *The Writer's Workout Book*, Art Peterson (1996) notes that good writers never just eat breakfast. "They munch on granola, wolf down hotcakes, savor Frosted Flakes, or gorge on jelly doughnuts" (p. 106). Peterson advises writers to work for this kind of specificity: "You should not settle for the general. Keep asking yourself, 'Like what?' 'What else?' 'What about it?'" (p. 106).

Choosing appropriate, precise words takes on new significance in an academic discipline like science where terminology may be specific to the topic or the field. This excerpted piece from a ninth grader demonstrates the exactness required when writing about a subject like bees (terminology is underscored for emphasis):

Bees are naturally busy <u>organisms</u>. . . .

Because of their natural aid to plant <u>reproduction by pollination,</u> bees are naturally an important part of many food chains and many life cycles. Without bees, the amount of available food for <u>primary consumers</u> will decrease dramatically and therefore affect <u>secondary and tertiary consumers,</u> causing food chains to collapse.

In order to perform these jobs that support and affect many other animals, bees live very industrious lives in <u>colonies</u>. Within these colonies, each bee has a specialized job, which include queens, workers, and drones. The Queen bee is a big female bee whose job is to lay eggs to create the next generation of bees as well as run the hive. Worker bees are female bees that are smaller than the queen, and their job is to do work around the colony that could include jobs like bringing in nectar from flowers. Drones are male bees that fertilize the Queen. They get driven out of the colony during winter to prevent them from eating all the food.

Despite being a critical component of the environments that they live in, many bees are being wiped out (nearly 1/3 of the nation's hives) by <u>Colony Collapse Disorder</u>. The causes of this <u>disorder</u> are things like <u>modern agriculture practices</u> and <u>parasites</u>. Practices such as plowing and tilling soil and pesticides as well as enemies of bees such as <u>microscopic mites</u>, diseases, and moths are the reasons for Colony Collapse Disorder. . . .

Certainly this writing features **precise words** with its use of terminology, and it serves as an example of increasingly **sophisticated** vocabulary. The CCSS put a strong emphasis on use of language, including several language tiers. CCSS Tier 2 words are "more likely to appear in written texts than in speech." Tier 2 words in this piece include *organism, reproduction by pollination, consumers, secondary, tertiary,* and *disorder,* among others. The piece also contains Tier 3 words, defined by CCSS as domain-specific words that are key to understanding new concepts: *colony, agricultural practices, microscopic, Colony Collapse Disorder.* It's worth noting that AWC descriptors, for example, **precise** and **sophisticated**, connect well with the vocabulary standards within the CCSS (CCSSO & NGA, 2010, Appendix A, p. 33).

Conventions

The conventions attribute describes how effectively the writing demonstrates age-appropriate control of usage, punctuation, spelling, capitalization, and paragraphing.

CONVENTIONS can cause more disagreement than any other writing attribute. Teachers don't always see eye-to-eye on their importance or where they fit into the scheme of things: Are conventions the *first* order of business or the *last*? To add to the confusion, we all have our personal list of no-nos, whether it's run-on sentences or misusing *there, their,* and *they're.*

The AWC is arranged so that CONVENTIONS are not the first consideration, just as in many classrooms teachers encourage students to hold off on correctness until they have something to correct. The idea is to get some thoughts down before editing for conventions. At the same time, conventions count. Indeed, a lack of conventions can interfere with the meaning of a piece.

Here we offer two illustrations. The first is an excerpt from a high school informative essay:

. . . Unlike other departments within the government, the Department of Defense is liable for providing the military forces needed to prevent war and protect the security of our country. Our veterans leave their families and put their lives on the line every day to protect our country. In deserts and swamps, removed from all the comforts of home, our soldiers work long hours in pressure-filled situations; Jonathan Pruden is one brave soldier that enjoys telling his story.

While in the infantry in Iraq, Pruden was victim to a roadside bombing resulting in one hundred seventy-three pieces of shrapnel in his body, a bullet through both legs, a large hole in his back, two burst eardrums, immobility in his left eye and arm, and a severely ruptured artery in his leg. The accident resulted in more than twenty surgeries in seven different hospitals. Pruden proclaimed that desperation to see his family again is what kept him alive. So many soldiers—brothers, sisters, aunts, uncles, moms, and dads—leave home to fight for our freedom, but never return. They pay with great sacrifice yet never collect. They come face to face with their fears and conquer them for our freedom and safety. . . .

This writing exhibits **outstanding control of age-appropriate standard writing conventions** and includes a **wide range of conventions intentionally used for stylistic effect,** for example, the use of dashes to set off a string of details. **Spelling, usage, punctuation, capitalization, and paragraph breaks are correct to the extent that almost no editing is needed.**

Now take a look at writing that is not as proficient. The following excerpt from a first draft written by a community college student demonstrates less control of age-appropriate conventions:

Sometimes it is a little annoying living by your family because they start to come by your house unexpectedly and eat your food. Like once I left and went out of town with my brother and my mom and I spent a whole year collecting coins in my big jar. When I made it back from my trip all of my coins were gone I was so upset. But other than that, I feel safe being around them. Even though they get on my last nerves at time I am safe when I walk out the door at night because I know I am around loving and caring family member.

This writing illustrates **a struggle with control of basic conventions.** It contains **errors in usage,** both pronoun and verb, and **punctuation,** both ending as well as internal. The writing requires **extensive editing.**

It matters that this writing comes from a community college student because the AWC specifies **control of age-appropriate standard writing conventions** across all grade levels. A postsecondary student should be able meet both the AWC standard and the CCSS standard, which is to "demonstrate command of the conventions of standard English grammar and usage when writing. . . . " and to "demonstrate command of the conventions of standard English capitalization, punctuation, and spelling when writing" (Council of Chief State School Officers [CCSSO] & the National Governors Association [NGA], 2016).

A FINAL NOTE ABOUT ATTRIBUTES

"There is no collection of words so perfect that once put on a page, they cannot be misinterpreted or misused." Former NWP research and evaluation director Paul LeMahieu would start off every NWP National Scoring Conference with this statement. And here it serves as a benediction. The AWC could be turned into a formula or checklist overnight. The attributes could be taught as a forced march. The flexibility represented in the AWC's continuum could be reduced to a set of hard-and-fast rules.

Now that the words are on the page, we look to teachers to avoid this type of reductionism. To that end, we will devote the next section of this book to stories about teachers who brought the AWC to their classrooms, enhancing and tailoring it to meet the needs and aspirations of their students.

CHAPTER 3

The AWC Goes to the Classroom

Who knew when the binder clip made its debut in 1910 that the world would invent so many uses for it? True, it admirably accomplishes its original mission of holding papers together. But its fans have invented so many more uses. These include emergency cuff links, cell phone car mount, money clip, bookmark, recipe card holder, cable catcher, razor safety cover, toothpaste tube squeezer, keychain, and easy eyeglass repair.

We use the lowly binder clip to illustrate the concept of a community of users: people who discover and share the benefits of a particular product. These users do not necessarily have anything else in common—background, training, or similar experiences. What binds them (excuse the pun) is the fact that they have used, tailored, or tweaked the same tool to serve various purposes.

In the case of the writing continuum, its community of users—teachers—has a long tradition of inventing advantageous solutions and improvements to a myriad of classroom challenges, from popping tennis balls on squeaky desk legs to teaching writers how to develop their ideas. Teachers are nothing if not resourceful. When it came to the AWC, many teachers decided to see what would happen if they moved this tool from a hotel ballroom where they were scoring student papers to the classroom where they were teaching live students. There is no consumer trial with more stringent demands than a trial with students. On the other hand, there was the possibility that the students themselves might become part of the community of AWC users, confident in how they write, in how they talk about writing, and in sharing their knowledge with other students.

What follows are the teachers' stories about their experiences as they used, adapted, scrutinized, tested, tossed around, and otherwise reinvented the AWC for their own classroom purposes. The stories illustrate how teachers and students—working individually and collectively—turned the AWC into a tool for teaching and learning, for understanding and improving writing, and for responding to and assessing a wide variety of genres. These are truthful stories; not every minute spent with the AWC is a minute made in heaven. They are also reflective stories told by teachers who don't mind sharing their uncertainties along with their moments of triumph. Every story features approaches to teaching rather than "surefire" lessons that somehow, no matter what they promise, do not suffice for every student. We are reminded of the eight-year-old whose father rented him a wet suit so he could swim in cold water. The suit was clearly sized and labeled for a child of a certain age, weight, and height. But as it turned out, the wet suit was ill-fitting in the case of this eight-year-old. Not only did it fail to protect the child from chill, but it made him self-conscious. "I feel like a marshmallow," he complained, looking down at the suit, loose and bloated with water.

We have tried to avoid the marshmallow effect in the stories that follow. Rather than rent out potentially ill-fitting lessons, we have analyzed the classroom experiences of the teachers and students to help readers who wish to alter the AWC for the right fit in their own classrooms.

USING THE AWC AS A FORMATIVE ASSESSMENT TOOL

Nikki Mathews is the only language arts teacher for more than 100 seventh graders in a middle school near Twin Falls, Idaho. She began teaching in 2000 and made her way to the Boise State Writing Project in the summer of 2007. As a veteran teacher, Mathews had a "been there—done that" relationship with rubrics before encountering the AWC:

> I was no stranger to rubrics. In fact, I had become quite skeptical of them. In the beginning of my teaching career, I used rubrics as summative assessments for the majority of my assignments. Rubrics seemed to be a la mode—everyone was using them.
>
> So, being the eager teacher that I am, I created rubrics for nearly every assignment. I had rubrics for short writing assignments, stories, even poems! Finally, out of frustration, I stopped using them because my students would not read my long extensive comments on the rubric I used for that assignment. When I gave the final assignments back to them, they only looked at the grade. I even saw some of the rubrics in the trash where students had tossed them while leaving my classroom. The following is a typical exchange that I had with students after I spent hours writing comments on each and every rubric for their final assignment.

> *Circa 2004: Conversation with student*

> *Student:* I can't believe I got a C on that poem!
> *Mrs. Mathews:* Did you read what I wrote on the rubric?
> *Student:* No, I didn't read it. I just know I got a C.

The rubrics, at least how I was using them, didn't help my students, and they were a lot of work for me. I remember having the following discussion with a parent on why his child received the grade he did on an assignment.

Circa 2005: Conversation with parent

Parent: Hey, why did my child get a C on his paper?

Mrs. Mathews: I wrote lots of comments on his rubric. It explained why. I believe he had a lot of punctuation errors and there was a problem with organization.

Parent: Oh, I didn't see that. I just know that I thought it was really good and he worked hard on it.

So what was happening to my rubrics? Why was I even bothering? They took a lot of time to create and they took a lot of time to grade. I decided it was time to get rid of the dastardly rubrics and discover a better way of grading. . . . They only complicated my grading process and the students had no interest in what the rubric said.[1]

Mathews had another bone to pick with rubrics. She found the state's holistic rubric "simplistic" and inadequate as a feedback mechanism for students to learn anything concrete about their performances on the required expository essay. The very fact that the state rubric focused solely on expository writing limited its usefulness in Mathew's view. She also noted that the wording regarding organization encouraged students to write a formulaic paper ("an introduction, body paragraphs, and a conclusion"), and the distinctions on the four-point scale seemed hazy in contrast to the AWC's positive, specific language about what is present in the writing at different score points.

Mathews first encountered the Analytic Writing Continuum at the NWP National Scoring Conference. "I remember thinking that this particular rubric would actually *help* my seventh graders write an essay for our state assessment!" That it could be used for any type of writing made sense to Mathews:

I wrote at the time, "I think it would be cool for a student to see his or her writing as a grand sculpture that is a work in progress." I hoped that my students could describe their writing pieces based on the attributes and find themselves—their strengths and weaknesses—on the continuum. I also hoped that I could move my writers along the continuum over the course of the year. Using the AWC rubric in this way to improve writing instruction *and* improve student writing versus to assess their writing would be a dramatic change to my former approach to teaching.

Inspired by NWP Michigan colleague Paula Diedrich, Mathews made her first move, adjusting the wording of the continuum to be age-appropriate for her students. She also included some wording from the 6 + 1 Trait Writing Model (ideas, organization, voice, word choice) because teachers in her school had received training in this model and, therefore, students were familiar with these terms.

Mathews introduced her seventh graders to her adapted continuum in the late fall. Once they were comfortable with the language, she handed them packets of anonymous papers to score in their table groups The idea was to help the students connect the language of the AWC to actual writing. Anonymous papers insured that the focus would be on the writing and not on the classmate who might have written it.

As she circulated the room, she listened in on their discussions and prompted them to look at the continuum:

Brett: The Eleanor of Aquitaine essay is definitely the best one!

Morgan: Yeah, I agree. This cyborg assassin essay looks like a first grader wrote it!

Mattie: I know! The Abraham Lincoln one is probably the 3 because it's pretty good too, but not as good as the Eleanor one. It's kind of boring.

Donna: This essay called "People" is hard to understand.

Mrs. Mathews: What qualities, according to the rubric make the Eleanor essay the best or a 4? Why is the Abraham Lincoln essay a 3? Explain your reasoning according to the rubric.

Shelby: Okay guys, I'll write it down. The Eleanor one definitely has more details and she has a lot of information about the topic. Where's that on the rubric?

Dallin: Content. It's really focused and specific.

Taylan: Yeah, and it's really organized and there's no confusing parts.

This brief dialogue illustrates a learning curve when peers talk together about writing. The early banter has a familiar ring to it—lots of personal opinion without much supporting evidence. Once the teacher intervened, however, the students turned to the AWC for some criteria. During the subsequent class discussion, students listed the attributes of the best essay and provided their own commentary, citing language from the writing itself. In the days that followed, students continued scoring essays and pinpointing their attributes or the areas that needed improvement. In other words, Mathews engaged her students in a classroom assessment process, an activity Davies and LeMahieu (2003) highly recommend:

For optimum learning to occur students need to be involved in the classroom assessment process. When students are involved in the assessment process they learn how to think about their learning and how to self-assess—key aspects of meta-cognition. Learners construct their own understandings therefore, learning how to learn—becoming an independent, self-directed, life long learner—involves learning how to assess and learning to use assessment information and insights to adjust learning behaviours and improve performance behaviours and improve performance. (p. 142)

Now it was her students' turn to write practice essays, as they'd always done in preparation for the state assessment. But this time around, Mathews revised her approach:

The AWC was changing my thinking about how rubrics can be used and made me realize how important *formative assessment* is with writing as opposed to *summative assessment*. . . . The rubric came after the fact. It had no meaning to my students. One of the wonderful aspects I love about the AWC is it is a fluid continuum that doesn't put writing pieces in nice tidy boxes or "coffins" if you will. It is not the end all. It is a *guide* for navigating writing.

When teachers like Mathews change their thinking about their practice and try out new approaches, most often they have some kind of sounding board—whether a colleague or a group of colleagues. Taking risks is one thing, but doing so while attending to all the other daily classroom demands is another. Mathews was preparing her students for the state assessment, even as she was trying out the AWC. She credits her local writing project's teacher inquiry group for supporting her as she ventured into unknown territory:

The meetings we had together for this research project were a critical part of my learning. After each meeting, I felt as though I was not the only one with a machete slashing through this vast jungle alone; I had more insight, direction, and encouragement than ever before. Even though we were all using the AWC differently in our classrooms, we were all in this boat together and that made all the difference to me. The important principle here is that teachers need what students need—a vision, a purpose, assistance over time, and a community of fellow learners to help them along the way.

Meeting with her inquiry group also prompted Mathews to assign fewer essays in order to have time for more instruction on the writing attributes. "We should do less to achieve more," Mathews discovered. "My students need time to write, reflect, and have active assistance in the process of writing and they also need a lot of feedback."

What Mathews wants for her students—"time to write, reflect, and have active assistance"—is exactly what Mathews herself needs as a teacher.

By engaging with colleagues in a teacher inquiry group, she gets the whole package: shared perspectives, mutual reflection, ongoing support, and lots of feedback. In the end, she has new insights about her teaching. According to Goswami, Lewis, Rutherford, and Waff (2009), it's those insights—finding out "if what we are teaching is serving the students under our care"—that motivate teachers to conduct classroom research:

> Are they learning—learning to read, write, think, imagine, invent, and create? In this era of abundant assessment, we know a lot about scores on tests, rankings, and percentiles; but all too often, too many of us are left not knowing if the students we teach are receiving enough of what they need to be great citizens, strong and productive members of the communities they inhabit who are able to make a decent living because they can think, write, and analyze their world. At the end of the day as teachers, we are often left wondering: Are we doing enough? How do we know? These are the essential questions that occupy the minds and hearts of so many of us when we walk into our classrooms. This is the reason to do teacher research: to document student learning—the kind of documentation that leads to answers to these essential questions. (p. 2)

Back in the classroom, Mathews' students wrote and revised their practice essays. At that point, Mathews invited them to work in self-chosen writing groups where they scored one another's papers and gave feedback based on the AWC. As she toured the room, she noticed the confidence with which her students reflected on their own and others' writing. In particular, she was impressed with the increasing quality of their comments to one another. She observed a group of boys, for example, "truly talented writers," challenging one another with clever words, an outgrowth of their study of DICTION. Another group of students focused on an especially promising introduction to an essay on Michael Phelps. No doubt they appreciated the topic, but they also had come to recognize a compelling opening as part of a paper's STRUCTURE. And then there was Shelby, who wrote the following to her teammate: "The voice in your essay is really, really good. You write like you are talking to a friend, and that's pretty sweet. The word choice is good too—they are clear, varied, precise." Then she suggested, "Make sure you have the right words for what you want to say. Maybe a little more interesting intro, too." In fact, many of Mathews' students were able to give each other specific suggestions using the AWC. Kody, for instance, told his buddy Colin that "he needs to focus on the reasons and details in his paragraphs."

These comments are a far cry from the standard-issue "it was good" that so many students rely on when they read another student's paper. But there's more going on here. Because Mathews gave class members time to take stock of their writing, her students assumed a more active role in their own learning, even telling her that they wanted to improve in diction and stance. "This feedback was invaluable to me because it shaped and informed my future instruction," Mathews explains, adding:

> It also made me realize the importance of *my* place in the classroom. It's not the rubric alone that motivates students to write; that responsibility is with me. . . . The AWC rubric is simply a paper by itself. It is up to the *teacher* to use it well.

So what happened when the seventh graders took the state assessment? Did they improve compared to their fifth-grade scores? Yes. But were the gains as astounding as Mathews had hoped? No:

> In March, after sharing the results of the state assessment with my students, I had them reflect on their scores, the rubric, and this question: "Explain what you learned about writing this year so far." Here are some of their comments:
> - "That my sentences need to be more fluent."
> - "That papers have voice."
> - "That we had to organize paragraphs."
> - "I learned a lot about the way you write, like to make a good essay it requires personality, describing words, stays on topic, and gives good details and examples."
> - "I learned that staying organized really helps staying focused on the paper."
> - "I learned how to punctuate better."
>
> What I found interesting about these comments was that I see threads of the AWC in most of them. Now my students were *naming* what they knew about writing using specific terms of the AWC! They were internalizing the rubric!
> By the end of the year, most of the writing I was receiving from my students was more focused, organized, included sentence fluency, stance, descriptive details, and they were getting better with conventions. Now, do I attribute *all* of this to the AWC? No, not completely. But, for the first time in my teaching career, I used a well-developed, carefully constructed rubric as a tool for *formative assessment* not only to prepare my students for the state assessment, but also to improve their writing. What I found was that it not only made a difference in my students' writing, but it changed my teaching practice as well.

There are some themes in this classroom story that will show up again in the stories to come:

- Even though Mathews had never used the AWC before (and had a dubious track record with rubrics in general), she made a plan for introducing the AWC to her students, using papers from unidentified writers.

- Mathews felt free to tailor the AWC language to suit the age of her students and their past experiences.
- She taught students to use the AWC language when they commented on one another's papers.
- She slowed down the pace, inviting students to reflect on and take charge of their learning.
- Mathews used her students' progress, performances, and reflections to plan her instruction.

Other teachers have also made discoveries about using the AWC to give feedback and build writers. Indiana seventh grade teacher Bonnie Stewart says that the AWC has helped her most in learning how to analyze her students' writing and then figure out how to move their writing along the continuum. Her experience with the AWC "focused me to look at the positive things in my students' writings instead of seeing only the negatives. When I talk to students, I tell them 'You're really strong in this. And now we're going to take this and build the others [attributes] around it'" (personal communication, June 18, 2009).

Missouri twelfth grade teacher Julie Sheerman encourages her students to use the language of the continuum during peer conferencing, but not to assign a numerical score. When she gives feedback on a paper, she takes a copy of the continuum and highlights where she sees a student's writing best fits, and in doing so, she uses the specific language for each attribute. "Students then set two goals for the next draft," Sheerman explains. "This process results in a different quality of revision" (personal communication, June 20, 2008).

Sheerman's use of the AWC for goal-setting may be one of the best moves for improving student writing. According to Gary Troia (2013), "setting goals enhances attention, motivation, and effort and facilitates strategic behavior (e.g., planning in advance of writing) through valuation of goal attainment" (p. 414). He goes on to explain the following:

> Research has demonstrated that goal setting improves writing skills in struggling writers (De La Paz, 2007; Graham et al., 1992; Graham, MacArthur, & Schwartz, 1995; Page-Voth & Graham, 1999; Schunk & Swartz, 1992). For goals to have the most beneficial impact on writing behavior and performance and to encourage students to marshal sufficient effort, they should be challenging (i.e., just beyond the student's current level of writing skill), proximal (i.e., attainable within a short period of time), concrete, and self-selected or collaboratively established (because real or perceived control boosts achievement motivation). (pp. 414–415)

Sheerman's approach capitalizes on all the aspects listed above: goals that are challenging and concrete, and that are self-selected, with collaboration during the teacher/student conference.

USING THE AWC AS A TOOL FOR TEACHING ABOUT CONTENT

Thirty-year veteran teacher Debbie Dehoney did not leap at the opportunity to attend the NWP National Scoring Conference, nor did she anticipate that she would learn anything there that might help her primary-grade students. She says, however, that her professional conscience "got the best of her," so she boarded a plane and hoped she was making the right decision. After the conference, an unexpected eye-opener, she began a journey with the AWC that led her to more places she never imagined.

Dehoney teaches in a Title I school in rural Kimberly, Idaho, population 3,400, where the majority of her second graders' parents work in agriculture or related businesses. According to Dehoney, "most students have chores to do with farming that have to be done before and after school each day" (personal communication, June 26, 2016).

Dehoney has high standards when it comes to her students and their writing. She wants second graders to be conscious of what and how they write. Intentional about purpose and audience. Versatile in tackling different genres. She also understands how second graders operate—an understanding that led her to focus her energies on one AWC attribute at a time:

> Since second graders always have a story to tell (usually about their dog, cat or some serious injustice that has been committed against them) and they have a tendency to go on and on about nothing, I chose to work on *Content* using the AWC bullets as a guide. If they are having content problems, is there a point in going into sentence fluency or organization for example?[2]

Dehoney began her AWC adventure by reading aloud several silly stories from children's literature in which "the characters find themselves in various situations that could be disastrous, but the day is saved when they do something out of the ordinary that is also very silly. Second graders do love nonsense! I used one of the stories, 'Dragon Gets By,' as the mentor text for the beginning of our study about content, with the AWC guiding us to what makes a story interesting and fun to read."

To help her students wrestle with content in their own writing, Dehoney made several decisive moves. First, she singled out the CONTENT attribute of the AWC and rewrote it in kid-friendly ("kidlish") language. Her goal was to give her students a "writer's vocabulary"—special words they could use when talking about their writing.

Then Dehoney put the special words to the test:

We took each story we read in those two weeks and compared it to the criteria in our revised (kidlish) Content attribute, answering *Yes* or *No* to each bullet. To be honest, I almost gave up. Even though the children knew the language and understood the bullets, I was getting only a little conversation and discussion (and for a class that liked to talk about anything and everything ALL THE TIME, it was very unusual that they didn't have something to say). I was hoping for more debate and not just yes and no answers, but I promised myself two weeks and I'm glad I did. I realized that I was trying to impose this on my time schedule not theirs! All of a sudden my students were beginning to use the language of the AWC. They began discussing, debating and rationalizing. If they didn't remember a word like *consistently* they would say, "you know teacher that word that means you do the same thing, the same way over and over again." What I realized and remembered was something Jeff Wilhelm taught me: "deep learning takes time and lots of practice."

Dehoney still had her work cut out for her. She wanted content but not the "on and on" stories she was used to getting with second graders. Interspersed with the reading, she and her students dove into a focus activity:

We constructed glasses out of cardboard tubes and called them our "focus glasses." We wore our "focus glasses," outside and I had the children look at trees, the building, playground equipment, etc. and describe what they saw through the glasses. Their peripheral vision was blocked so they could only see straight ahead. I explained that this is what we want our writing to look like. We want it to stay on the topic and not wander all over the place. (These focus glasses turned out to be a good thing. I started to use them when the kids got into telling one of their stories that never end! I would just say "time to put on your focus glasses." We cut 15 minutes off of show and tell time with this great discovery!)

Dehoney is nothing if not fearless. First the focus glasses. Then offering her own writing for her students to see and compare with the AWC Content descriptors. Her students were not shy about responding: "Now don't get mad teacher, but you describe your dog Maggie as a big white dog, maybe you could tell how white, like snow white, or as white as a big puffy clouds white? How big is Maggie, is she as big as a pony or a deer or maybe a baby calf?"

Ultimately, students brought their own drafts to conference with Dehoney, using the Content attribute and following a specific agenda:

1. Student reads the piece aloud.
2. Dehoney comments or asks questions for understanding.
3. Student and teacher review the content score 6 together.
4. Student and teacher score the piece answering "yes" or "no."
5. Student and teacher compare scores and discuss reasons for each "yes" or "no."
6. Both make suggestions for the piece.
7. Student decides whether to publish.

Dehoney explains this last item about publishing:

> I always let my students decide what pieces they want to publish. Second graders think everything they write is ready for the best sellers list! But I do give them some guidelines in trying to decide if the piece they wrote is something they should publish. For example, have you done your best work? Could you possibly (in the future) write another chapter to this story? Is it something you want to keep forever? Who do you hope your audience will be for the finished product?

What follows is an example of Dehoney's conference agenda, beginning with a piece of writing by a young student, Andrew, and then Dehoney's response. Note that Dehoney sticks with CONTENT, resisting any temptation to touch on other attributes of good writing, but rather focusing on the places in the draft that need more development:

Andrew's story: Once I got a cut. I was riding my bike between the fence and my mom's car. I crashed into my mom's car. It was about a 14 inch cut. It was on my leg. I had to wear a band aide. My gramma, papa, mom and dad was there.

Conference with Andrew: "Andrew, this is a great story; I hope your cut healed fast! How did you crash again? Oh, you were going too fast riding between the car and the fence and you lost your balance and hit your mom's car. Did you hurt the car? (chuckle) Your cut was pretty big; did it take a lot of Band-Aids? 10 of them! WOW! That's a lot of Band-Aids. Well, Andrew, let's take a look at the Content bullets and review them quickly so we both understand what we are going to talk about." I then handed Andrew a copy of the bullets and I took one. We each answered "yes" or "no" to each bullet and then compared answers and discussed why we answered each bullet as we did.

Teacher and student review content attribute: Figure 3.1 summarizes the next part of the conference, during which Dehoney and Andrew evaluate the piece for its strengths and for areas to improve.

Figure 3.1. Teacher and Student Review Content Attribute

CRITERIA	MY EVALUATION		ANDREW'S SELF-EVALUATION	
AWC CONTENT Attributes	Yes/No	My Response to Andrew's First Draft	Yes/No	Andrew's Response to His First Draft
Clear (Do you understand the story?) and always focused (Stays with the topic); exceptionally (Not just good, but great!) well-shaped and -connected (The story makes sense).	No	Your story is clear until you talk about your family. I'm confused when I read that part.	No	I did talk about getting hurt, but I didn't tell how old I was or what I was doing to get hurt.
Reflects outstanding control and development of ideas and content. (The author did the very best job at making the story funny, sad, or real.)	No	I wanted to know more details about the accident and when, how and why it happened.	No	I coulda made the story a lot more real if I described all the blood all over the place.
Contains ideas that consistently and fully support and/or enhance the central theme or topic— well-developed details, reasons, examples, evidence, anecdotes, events, and or descriptions. (The author did the very best job at telling you everything you needed to know using exact details, examples, or descriptions so that you could actually see in your mind what they were trying to say.)	No	Again I want to know more: How did you feel? Did you cry? What kind of bike were you riding? Where were you going?	No	Oops, I didn't put in there that my mom's car was new and I hadn't seen it much yet. I didn't tell what everyone else was doing like my dad and papa. Did you know that we live in the country and we have a road between my house and my gramma's. I don't even have to go on the real road ever.

Figure 3.1. Teacher and Student Review Content Attribute

CRITERIA	MY EVALUATION		ANDREW'S SELF-EVALUATION	
AWC CONTENT Attributes	Yes/No	My Response to Andrew's First Draft	Yes/No	Andrew's Response to His First Draft
Ideas are consistently purposeful, specific, and often creative. (The author used ideas in the story that made sense and made you think, "Why didn't I think of that?")	No	Can you tell me more about where the story takes place?	No	I don't think I was creative and this bullet is hard for me to understand.

Note: "Kidlish" appears in parentheses.

Andrew's rewrite: One day when I was 3 or 4 years old, I was riding my bike home from my gramma's house, she lives next door but it's a quarter of a mile away. We have a road that connects our houses so I don't have to ride on the real road. It was evening and my gramma was riding with me on her red bike. My gramma stopped to talk to my mom who was in the vegetable garden. My gramma told my mom she liked her new car cause it was red like her bike. I listened for a minute and then I went to put my bike away. I had to ride between the back fence and my mom's new car. I really liked our new red car and I was looking at it really hard and all of a sudden I fell off my bike. I scraped my knee clear down to my ankle. It took 10 band aides to patch it up. It hurt bad, but I thought I looked really cool with all those band aides on! I never wanted to take them off.

Andrew's second draft is much longer than the first and far more developed. In particular, the ideas are now **consistently purposeful, specific, and often creative,** with details that explain how the narrator fell, at what age, and how many Band-Aids it took to patch him up. The revised piece is also **well-shaped and connected** as it describes the events that led up to the accident.

During the year, Dehoney discovered students using the rubric with one another to talk about their own writing. Even better, their writer's notebooks reflected a change in the quality of the content:

For example, one entry in Jenna's notebook at the beginning of the year said, "We went for ice cream with my grandma in her new car last night. It was fun."

In October the entry in Jenna's notebook said, "We got a huge surprise last night! My dad brought home a new car for our family. It is dark green like the evergreen trees outside the school and the inside is brown, well really tan like your skin gets in the summer when you forget to wear sunscreen. I got to ride in the front seat!"

Many of the notebooks began showing 2–3 entries a day written on [students'] own time, with a conscious effort . . . instead of an afterthought of "Oh Mrs. Dehoney will expect to see an entry in my writer's notebook, I better write something."

But the enterprise was not without its frustrations. Dehoney noted over and over again the passage of time—more than three weeks—and the sheer energy it took to help her students catch on. She had to scrap her plans to introduce a different part of the continuum each quarter. Too much, too soon, she realized. That said, Dehoney was impressed that the class—including a smattering of English learners and special needs students—did well with the CONTENT attribute.

Another plus for Dehoney was the way the AWC "linked all the knowledge and theories I had gathered over the years." For example, she was able to connect reading and writing with the AWC, beginning with a mentor text and then working through a tried-and-true writing process, including drafting, conferencing, revising, and, in some cases, publishing. Dehoney cites the AWC as "the inspiration" but also as "something tangible" that fit into the teaching approach she had designed over the years.

USING THE AWC TO TEACH REVISION

The following scene, described by middle school teacher Denise Mumm, occurred at the end of the school year after her students had worked with the AWC. Mumm, a 23-year veteran, is the sole teacher of eighth graders in her rural school and a teacher consultant with the Boise State Writing Project.

I stand near the bookshelf in the library, observing my students as they work at the computers. Conversations buzz through the air, and I, ever the disciplinarian, am looking for the culprit: that off-task student discussing who he or she has a crush on. But as I try to zero in on the trouble maker, I can't detect any conversations that are not about the writing pieces! Everyone is talking about their ideas or reading what they just wrote to a neighbor.

I notice a tall, gangly boy, Daniel, heading down the row of computers to get to Eddie's station. I move closer, getting ready to pounce and get him back on task. But Daniel leans over Eddie's shoulder, reading his friend's draft. "How can I get rid of these linking verbs?"

Eddie asks. A conversation ensues about diction and how to get more active verbs into the writing piece. There is laughter and there are suggestions. Then Daniel, making sure he touches everyone on his way, wanders back to his station and continues his work.[3]

This student conversation might not have happened if Mumm had stayed with her first reaction to the AWC when she encountered it at the 2009 NWP National Scoring Conference. She was not impressed. Nor did she think it contained any magical properties that would enhance the writing of her students. Her experiences with the state writing assessment made her skeptical: "A writing rubric is a rubric is a rubric. Change the name, tweak it a bit, and off we go, again."

Mumm's participation in her site's teacher inquiry group was the impetus for giving the AWC a try. Concerned about her English learners, Mumm decided to concentrate on the areas of SENTENCE FLUENCY and DICTION— areas that particularly challenged them. With each subsequent exercise or writing assignment, she asked her students "why they did what they did, how they used what I taught, and what they learned."

When the days are good in teaching, they are very, very good and when they are bad, well, they can be horrid. So it was for Mumm. She experienced sheer elation during one of her lessons on SENTENCE FLUENCY:

> I was teaching a mini-unit on phrases to my 2nd quarter writing class. After a few class periods and a lot of modeling and mentoring, most of my students could successfully add participle phrases to their sentences as introductory elements or interrupters. One activity we did had students writing a quick, bland paragraph, and then exchanging papers with a partner across the room. Next they had to add participle phrase to improve the sentence fluency (improving flow, using effective phrasing, varying sentences in length, showing a relationship between sentences) of the piece of writing. Kids were totally engaged in this exercise! They were having fun adding the phrases; they were getting feedback from tablemates, and if they were unsure of their work, they were getting help from peers or their hands would fly in the air to get my assistance. They eagerly shared their writing when we had finished.
>
> What a great day that was in my classroom! I was on top of my game, the pinnacle of my teaching career! I had put together all the pieces that promoted understanding: My students were engaged in the social nature of engaged learning; they were given time to explore the concept; they were revising; and they were on their way to understanding the attribute of sentence fluency and how using a phrase structure as a tool can improve their writing. I wrote in my reflective journal that day:

WOW LESSON! Kids love this! They were laughing, sharing and trying to use the correct form. Frank (who NEVER volunteers information in class) responded in a whole group discussion afterward that "we need phrases to add description." Why was this so much better than my 3rd quarter lesson? I had purpose for the writing this time!

But then came a dry spell. Mumm had her eye on the upcoming state assessment with its various challenges, one of them being gerund and infinitive phrases. More than once Mumm cautioned her students, "A gerund phrase acts like a noun," and "an infinitive phrase may be a noun or adjective or adverb."

During this phase of instruction, she and her students became increasingly frustrated. "Why do we have to learn this?" her students wailed. And then came the inevitable: "This is boring!" "How does this help us to be better writers?"

Mumm had an epiphany, but not before she admonished her complaining eighth graders that they needed to know how all the parts of a sentence work "so they wouldn't confuse their verbs." She heard herself say the words. She looked hard at her class, wilting before her eyes. And then she made the leap:

I, as a writer, do not purposefully use gerunds and infinitives. Why was I making my students? The problem was that I was trying to teach a grammatical structure without a real purpose in their writing. This was a huge "aha" moment for me. This is when I finally let go of the traditional grammar that I had been teaching, which was on the ISAT that we were scheduled to take at the end of the year. It was the pressure of this high-stakes assessment that was driving my push for teaching the infinitives and gerunds: not that they were tools students could use to make their writing better.

It's not uncommon, of course, for teachers to weed out their curriculum by eliminating lessons that have gone awry. But in Mumm's case, the decision to dump gerunds and infinitives was informed by her experience as a writer, by her careful watching and listening to her students, and by dipping into the AWC as a center for her instruction. "Using the AWC to focus my writing instruction showed me that not all grammatical structures need to be taught in order for students to move up the continuum in diction and sentence fluency." In fact, the AWC does not name traditional grammar as an attribute of good writing, focusing instead on conventions, including spelling, usage, punctuation, and paragraph breaks. The grammatical terms *verbs*, *nouns*, and *modifiers* show up in the DICTION attribute as words that, when lively and precise, will add depth and specificity to the writing.

Whether or not to explicitly teach grammar remains a debate among teachers. In their report, *Writing Next: Effective Strategies to Improve Writing of Adolescents in Middle and High Schools*, Graham and Perin (2007) reviewed studies of grammar instruction that included of parts of speech and sentence structure:

> The meta-analysis found an effect for this type of instruction for students across the full range of ability, but surprisingly, this effect was negative. This negative effect was small, but it was statistically significant, indicating that traditional grammar instruction is unlikely to help improve the quality of students' writing. (p. 21)

After her epiphany about teaching gerunds and infinitives, Mumm focused on how to help students with revision: "Instead of beginning a lesson with a blank board and generating our ideas about good diction or sentence fluency, I began with a piece of student writing and used writer's tools like phrases and clauses to show how to improve sentence fluency. I was now modeling how to improve writing instead of just telling students to improve their writing, and student writing improved." The following is an example of a first draft of student writing and the carefully revised final draft:

First Draft

How would you like to fly? Well I can tell you how! Just fall in the hands of evil scientists who do genetic experiments in children. If you love being chased by wolf men who are trying to kill you, locked in a cage, electrocuted, and /or killed during testing, then this method is definitely for you. Now, seriously, no one wants that except for a suicidal maniac, but that is what happened to the characters in the book Maximum Ride.

Final Draft

How would you like to soar through the air like a hawk using a pair of wings genetically attached to your body? Well, I can tell you how! Just fall into the hands of villainous-but-possibly-good-intentioned scientists who conduct genetic experiments on infants and children. If you love being stalked by wolf men who, by the way, are attempting to cut your life short, locked up in a cage, electrocuted, and /or killed during testing, then this method is definitely for you. Now, seriously, not one living thing on this planet that has a sane mind fantasizes about becoming a lab rat, except for a suicidal maniac, of course, but the characters in the series Maximum Ride had to endure these hardships anyway.

Mumm's modeling of SENTENCE FLUENCY paid off, as illustrated here in both the first and second drafts, which feature a combination of shorter and longer sentences and include a question and exclamation. When it comes to DICTION, the second draft takes off with **vivid words** and phrases, **lively verbs and precise nouns, figurative language** ("sail through the air like a hawk"), and some nice eighth-grade touches that are **creative and/or sophisticated:** "villainous-but-possibly-good-intentioned scientists." While either draft has merit, the second draft demonstrates a purposeful reworking of the piece. In the following reflection, the student writer describes a deepening understanding of revision:

> In the past, I put my ideas down on paper and called it good. I didn't think about how the words went on the page or what kind of words went on the page. A final draft was just a neater version of the rough one. Now, a final draft is a changed version of the rough one. It's revised, and sometimes the main idea or concept of the story is the only thing that remains. I focus on diction and vivid verbs. I try to make sure my sentence beginnings are varied.

When students can assess their own work as this young writer has done, the quality of their writing improves. In their report, *Informing Writing: The Benefits of Formative Assessment,* Graham, Harris, and Herbert (2011) explain:

> Teaching students how to assess their own writing has a positive and statistically significant effect on how effectively students convey thoughts and ideas through writing. . . . Self-evaluation procedures ranged from teaching students to use a rubric to assess the merits of specific features of their writing (e.g., ideation, organization, voice, vocabulary, sentence formation, and conventions) to teaching specific strategies for evaluating a first draft of a paper for substantive (e.g., clarity) or mechanical (e.g., misspelled words) lapses to teaching students how to detect mismatches between what they intended to say and what they wrote.
>
> Self-evaluation of writing had a consistently positive impact on the quality of students' writing. These gains occurred for students in grades three to twelve. (pp. 18–19)

Mumm, too, did some self-evaluation about her experience with the AWC. First, she promises herself that "any grammar instruction I do in my classroom will be in the context of students' actual writing and in service of teaching my writers tools they can use to become expert writers. These lessons will support the attributes of the AWC, and they will be grounded in good research and theory." But the focus and content of her teaching are not the only issues. Mumm offers another insight, one that brings up the age-old conflict for teachers: how to divvy up time, which always seems to be in short supply.

> When I was frustrated with the quality of student papers, I often thought that it was because I had done a poor job of instruction, or that I had not scaffolded a particularly difficult concept. But as my end-of-the-year interviews pointed out, most of the time it was because I did not give my students time to do the writing. One student I interviewed related her success on a certain piece of writing because "You gave us time in class to work on this." Another student wrote that she was "a better writer because she [Mumm] allowed us a lot of time to write."

Time is one of the elements that allows students to have control over their writing. Given time, and the support of peers and teacher, students produced a far better quality of writing. As one student, Bob, notes, " . . . also having time to revise the essay really helped. If I could do that on every piece of writing then maybe I could be an expert writer."

As for the AWC itself, Mumm has changed her mind about its usefulness:

> I didn't think the AWC was such a big deal last August when I was first introduced to it, but it ended up focusing writing instruction in my classroom. It acted as a natural scaffold for students, taking writers from where they were and moving them up the scale.

USING THE AWC TO FOCUS INSTRUCTION

How does a teacher who majored in math and science teach fourth graders how to write? For Jolene Hetherington, with 20 years of teaching under her belt, this question still looms large. Hetherington teaches in a rural school district in the middle of Michigan's Upper Peninsula where 45% of the students receive either free or reduced price lunch:

> I did not have a background in writing. I read student work and gave it a grade based on arbitrary criteria. I was not happy with the results so I decided to make up my own rubrics for writing assignments such as letters to authors, poetry, narrative stories, and science/social studies research papers. I struggled with making up criteria and point values for each writing assignment and still felt there was something missing both for myself as the evaluator and my students as learners. It became somewhat easier after I attended the Upper Peninsula Writing Project Summer Institute in 2003 where I developed my own writing skills and was able to learn from other teachers about assessing writing.[4]

In 2008, Hetherington found herself in Marquette, Michigan, at her writing project's advanced institute, where she learned about the AWC. Afterward, she used it as the basis for grading her students' writing, but not initially as a teaching tool. "I was in a steep learning curve myself. But I still wondered how using the AWC as a teaching tool could affect my students' learning. I had heard from other teachers their results of using an adapted AWC rubric in their classrooms." Being part of an action research group a year later was the impetus for Hetherington to give the AWC its second life in her classroom.

As we all know, much of what teachers teach—whether they like it or not—is determined by standards and assessments. Hetherington is no exception. She began her year by having her students read short fantasy books to meet a state grade-level content expectation. Along the way, Hetherington used the AWC to point out features of CONTENT and STRUCTURE. By the time students wrote their own fantasy stories, these attributes seem to have taken hold. "I felt the quality of the stories was better than past years . . . The stories seemed more alive than flat . . . They [students] also moved beyond the list-like singsong stories that have been prevalent in years past. Even my students who struggle with writing were successful in adding some conversation to their stories."

The AWC served Hetherington in yet another way. She had students read their rough drafts aloud to the whole class. Students discussed what they liked about the drafts, then asked questions and made suggestions, for example: "It would be better if her dad didn't save her. It would be better if she found her own way home. It would make your story longer and have more detail." In fact, the word *detail* popped up everywhere. Students pointed out that readers of their stories needed details to continue reading with interest. In their written self-evaluations, students commented: "I put a lot of work in my writing and a lot of details" and "I am good at making up *ideas*." This attention to content in both the composing and revision stages made a significant difference to the students' writing but also to their understanding of how to improve their writing.

Hetherington adapted the continuum to accommodate her fourth graders, and she also invited them to tell her the words that confused them: " . . . students did not know what the words *relevant, thoroughly,* and *exceptionally* meant. They turned those words into kidlish. So *relevant* became *has to do with the topic, thoroughly* changed to *totally,* and *exceptionally* evolved into *all* or *perfectly.*"

Hetherington also decided to stretch her luck with the AWC. Like the scientist she is, she wanted her students to look through a microscope at what writers do and at what writers are *supposed* to do in order to improve. That's when she pulled out some of her favorite science books, including *Explore the Desert, Icebergs and Glaciers,* and *Life in the Rainforest,* to show her students another kind of writing:

We spent a long time discussing colors of automobiles. That caught the attention of quite of few of my boys. We discussed how red means one specific color and then brainstormed other types of reds we could use. Then we transformed that into a discussion of how to be more specific when discussing animals.

These additional lessons on specificity with science texts and a nod to car lovers in the class proved to be worthwhile:

Science responses became more complete, longer, and more detailed than in previous years. For example, on the following test item: "Explain why the duck-billed platypus is considered a mammal. Then, tell why it is different from most other mammals," Mary responded, "The duck billed platypus is considered a mammal because it has fur and it drinks milk from its mother. It is different than most other mammals because it lives half the time in the water and it lays eggs on land and because it looks like a duck/bird but it's a mammal."

This test item short answer is **clear and consistently focused**. It exhibits details that **consistently and fully support the central topic** that the platypus is different from most other mammals, including information about where the platypus lives, how it reproduces, and what it looks like. "In past years," says Hetherington, "I would have gotten responses like 'because a duck billed platypus has part duck and part beaver and it has fur.'" So students in this class have embraced the idea of details, whether writing a story or responding to a test question. The potential for students to transfer their learning about an attribute from one kind of writing to another is an advantage of using the AWC.

Hetherington surveyed her students five times during the year as part of her action research. Initially, her students pointed to superficial features like penmanship when asked what good writing looks like. Gradually, they came up with more informed responses:

Jason wrote, "Good writing looks like a piece of writing that makes sense and has good excellent detail that makes me read on." "When it's a good paper, it has a beginning, middle, and end. It also has good word choice and has a lot of interesting details that capture the reader's attention," responded Autumn. When asked how their writing had improved over the year, the students overwhelmingly responded, "adding good, solid details" and "longer stories."

   On the subject of how the rubrics helped to improve your writing, Autumn wrote, "The rubrics help me think more." Cole stated, "They give me tips so I can use them in writing." "I know my standards. I see what I need," responded Sara. Katie replied, "Well, it tells me how I can improve it or how I can make it better by adding stuff to it."

Throughout her action research, Hetherington stressed the fact that she was diving into deep, unfamiliar waters when she took on the AWC as a teaching tool. Whether it was her training in science or her sheer determination to learn how to operate in a new field, she tested the tool for its relevance to her classroom and got positive results:

> The rubric helped me focus on what was in the writing in front of me. That led to lesson development based on my students' needs and to score what was present in their papers and not grade what was not there.

USING THE AWC TO TEACH RELUCTANT OR OTHERWISE "OUT OF THE BOX" STUDENTS

Kay Faile was teaching sophomores, juniors, and seniors in an alternative school when she first encountered the AWC in a teacher inquiry group at Texas State University. Looking at the six attributes and the six-point scale, she said out loud, "Now this is something I can use!" Having experienced little success with "end-of-the-line rubrics," designed to be used solely as final assessments, she appreciated the multiple dimensions of the AWC that allowed more precision in assessing where students were at various points in the process. "My students can be all over the map with content and diction; the flexibility fits my kids because they are all out of the box. That's why they are at risk."[5]

"I have non-writers," Faile explained. "They put up their hands and say, 'Just don't go there; I don't write.' My students have been told so many times that they can't write that they just don't want to do it anymore." With the AWC, Faile showed them that even though they may be low in one attribute, each of them had a more positive attribute to hang onto.

> So I now meet my students where they are, and the rubric is first and foremost. . . . It hit me one night like a lightning bolt. I used to bleed all over the papers, all over. So when that hit me you can't do that anymore. You have got to get rid of all of that. This is their writing. It's a personal thing; you must make it personal. And the Analytic Writing Continuum can help you do that. You can make this personal because if you teach them how to use that instrument, they will begin to be able to look and see where they are on their own and want to pull themselves up.

Faile delivered the AWC straight up: "I don't change anything. I use it as it is for all my students." In fact, she told her students they had the same brains as college students and the same ability to set their own course. But still her students—and thousands of others like them—were missing the part of the puzzle that would lead them to better writing:

> . . . not only do they not know what works in their paper, they don't know how to name or identify it. So how in the world can they practice it and understand how it works in the paper? So I said, "Okay, we're going to identify what works in a paper. We're going to name what that is and then we'll practice it." So we began to talk that way.
>
> I even developed little scripts, because I thought they need to understand the language and they need to use it in the correct way. So for each attribute I developed a little script and they would sit in groups of three and work from specific directions: "Go through and look for these things about content, and then you're going to tell me what you think works." And that's how we started. Then we would proceed through the continuum with each one of the attributes.

First Faile's students examined sample papers from the Internet. One attribute at a time, they learned to talk about the writing of others, then their own writing, and finally the writing of classmates. They practiced scoring in small groups. They scored, revealed their scores, and compared them—just as scorers do when calibrating at a scoring conference. In groups, they presented their scores and rationales to the class.

> I have the luxury of a block schedule, 90 minutes with my kids, and I can take eight weeks to solidly work with them on writing in the beginning of the year, and then throughout the year we play a game I call "Are You as Smart as a Professional Scorer?" I have the AWC on a flip chart. We get in our groups. I have a table with papers. "Pick up a paper and score it with your buddy."
>
> And then we say all our answers. And I will hear conversations like, "See, told you. See, I told you it was funny, and that's more difficult to write." "Didn't you get what this means . . . ?" And now I hear conversations, I never, ever, ever heard before about writing.
>
> And then they say, "Can we write? When can *we* write?" I was like holy cow! It just makes you excited about writing and you no longer go "Oh gosh, we're going to have to drag them screaming." Now it's, "Can we write, when can we?"

During her teacher/student conferences, Faile used the AWC to help her students become more intentional writers. For example, in conferring with exasperated students about their sentence fragments, she took them through the standard subject/verb lesson with a different outcome:

"Do you know what this is? They'll just kind of stare at me. And I'll say, "Do you know what this is?" I'll point to a fragment.

And they'll say, "Well, it's a sentence."

And I'll say, "Well, does it have a subject, does it?"—and we get to fragment. Then I'll say, "So fragments are not complete sentences and don't always work in certain places in your paper." Then I may say, "But guess what, listen to me read it and you will hear that this fragment works where you have decided to place it. See, because you used it to emphasize your point, it made me as a reader stop and think.

And so they'll say, "Oh, so I can do that."

And I can say, "You really have something that a lot of kids don't get for a long time, you've got it already."

Faile saw her students take ownership of their writing. She left their papers unmarked. "I'd give the paper to them and say, 'I want you to tell me what works. Here's the highlighter.'" In conferences or in class settings, Faile's students spoke about their writing, naming its features and talking about what they were trying to accomplish with each piece. For Faile, these were pinnacle moments: "It's just so cool when I can see a kid who really is struggling and I can say, 'You're the writer, you're the author so you tell me. I don't know what you want. You've got to tell me.' It's just excited me in a way that I never felt about writing before" (personal communication, January 14, 2014).

LESSONS LEARNED FROM THE CLASSROOM

The teachers whose stories we feature here do not share the same students or identical experiences with the AWC. Faile, for one, had no reservations about jumping right in—"now this is something I can use!"—while others felt more cautious about the AWC, having been burned by rubrics in the past or questioning whether this particular tool would be right for their classrooms. With the exception of Faile, who used the rubric "straight up," the teachers made adaptations that better aligned the AWC with their own contexts. In every case, these teachers provide a model for bringing any tool into the classroom: Question it. Experiment with it. Stretch and tailor it. Whether or not the tool makes sense as is or needs a significant amount of tweaking, its purpose and the standard for using it are to improve teaching and learning.

None of the teachers, it seems, anticipated the amount of time it would take to teach students how to use the AWC in a way that would improve their writing and their attitudes toward writing. This lesson may stand out as the most pertinent. There are few shortcuts when it comes to teaching students how to get better at one of the most challenging intellectual activities of all—writing. But as Faile pointed out, unless students can name and identify what they are doing when they write, they have no means of progressing. Instead, they tread water, try to keep their noses up, and hope for the best. No wonder so many students tag themselves as poor writers and give up.

At the time these teachers used the AWC in their classrooms, they had no crystal ball that forecast the arrival of the Common Core State Standards. However, they provide classroom examples that mirror the standards: In every case, teachers and students "collaborate" in various ways, whether to help compose, give feedback, or revise. In every case, teachers support students in "planning, revising, editing, rewriting." The teachers emphasize gathering "relevant information for content" and put a premium on "revision"—all of this with the AWC as a tool.

Finally, our community of users did not throw in the towel even on the worst days when forward progress with the AWC was elusive or missing altogether. To their great credit, they stayed the course and now are able to pass along some other lessons about how to use the AWC:

- Teach students to name and identify qualities of writing. Using a common language guides students when they give one another feedback and when they revise their own writing. High school teacher Julie Sheerman comments that the language helps students to locate both strengths and areas for improvement.
- Focus lessons on what will help students move forward as writers. Teach from the students' writing and from "where they are."
- Observe students. Listen to their conversations about writing.
- Ask them to tell you about their progress.
- Look at writing first for what is present, for strengths to build on.
- Build a classroom community of writers in which growth and improvement are within a student's control.
- Enjoy teaching writing.

CHAPTER 4

Putting the AWC to Work
in Your Backyard

The teachers we encountered in the last chapter designed their own action research projects—ones that were germane to their professional needs and the needs of their students. Avoiding the quick fix or the set-in-stone program, they followed an inquiry path that made sense to them and adjusted their initial focus as they went along. They scoured their students' work for signs of improvement and dared to ask these students what *they* thought about their writing, their progress, and this new AWC. Rather than shut their classroom doors to the peering eyes of their colleagues, they collaborated with other teachers who were interested in the teaching of writing and writing assessment and in how one can boost the other. Their willingness to work together brought about significant changes in their teaching and their students' writing performances:

> Any teacher who has been part of a successful collaboration with a friend, on a grade level team, or in an inquiry group, knows that two minds are more than twice as good as one. . . . A research group whose members share a commitment to looking closely at their practice, at themselves, and at the cultural perspectives they bring to their work can challenge group member's assumptions, spark ideas, and instigate improvements in practice. (Friedrich, Simons, & Tateishi, 2005, p. 125)

Both researchers and teachers have studied and written about teacher inquiry (also called teacher research and action research or some combination). A group of Northern Virginia teachers came up with their own definition of teacher research as inquiry that is "intentional, systematic, public, voluntary, ethical and contextual" (Mohr, Rogers, Sanford, Nocerino, MacLean, & Clawson, 2003, p. 23). These authors also describe teacher research as inclusive:

> It is conducted by preservice and beginning as well as experienced teachers, and it is of use to all teachers who wish to examine their practice, regardless of their level of expertise about teaching or research. (p. 25)

One question is why busy teachers would want to do yet one more thing. In their book *What Works: A Practical Guide for Teacher Research*, Chiseri-Strater and Sunstein (2006) describe teachers as "lifelong learners, continual questioners; otherwise, we wouldn't have chosen to spend our adulthood in school" (p. xvii). The authors see great value in conducting classroom research:

> Systematic inquiry, often called "action research" or "teacher research" offers the opportunity to answer questions for ourselves about our classrooms, our curriculum, and our students' learning. Classroom studies help us resist pre-packaged, laminated, hole-punched, "teacher-proof" curricula, attitudes about "teaching-to-the-test," and so many of the administrative mandates that oppress us. As we carry out research plans with our students, we sharpen our powers for understanding them and ourselves as learners. (pp. xvii–xviii)

As inclusive and valuable as it sounds, teacher research is still an undertaking. What might be the one ingredient that would encourage a teacher to take on a research project and stick with it? Teacher Paula Diedrich, who led the AWC action research group, offers this answer:

> I tried in the past to do inquiry in my classroom. When it's just me, I'm not as motivated. It's like quitting smoking. You have to tell people you're going to do it. And then you have to give each other progress reports. During our inquiry, we kept asking, "What are we learning from this experience?" even when things aren't going well. When we could see improvement or had an "aha" day, our successes helped us continue on. When we were having a "nothing went right" day, we had the courage to go on because of the group.[1]

In this chapter, we explore what made the AWC action research group successful and then we examine several scenarios for using the AWC in professional development. What characterizes both the inquiry and professional development examples is that in each, teachers look to one another for leadership, motivation, and insights. We also put these two professional activities together because they are so intertwined. Both involve teacher learning from research and practice, problem solving, sharing knowledge, and reflecting.

THE AWC AS AN INQUIRY TOOL

In some cases, the teachers who participated in the AWC inquiry group lived thousands of miles apart. What ultimately brought them together was an AWC scoring session in Chicago, where Frank Dehoney from Boise, Idaho, met Paula Diedrich from Marquette, Michigan. Dehoney thought Diedrich would be just the right person to work with teachers in his area to launch the AWC and see what it could do to improve student writing. Diedrich had led a professional development session at her writing project site, but nothing, she thought, that prepared her to work with teachers out West. According to Diedrich, "I kept saying to Frank that someone else should do this, but he was adamant. He thought the AWC was powerful and wanted to bring it to his writing project site."

Diedrich met with a small group of six Boise teachers in August. For three days she walked them through the AWC, teaching them the ins and outs of how it worked for scoring papers, and then talking about how they might use it in their classrooms. Afterward, the NWP director of research, Paul LeMahieu, encouraged Diedrich to lead this group in an action research project. Local writing project director Jeffrey Wilhelm offered his guidance as needed. The goal was to use the AWC to deepen understanding of the teaching of writing. As nervous as Diedrich was about "leading this wonderful group of teachers down the wrong path," she agreed to lead the project and to conduct her own inquiry along the way.

This story provides an important guideline for setting up an inquiry group. These group members shared a common aspiration to improve their teaching of writing, in this case by bringing the AWC into their classrooms. They made some other agreements as well. According to Diedrich, "we were willing to let our students in on the fact that we weren't sure exactly what we would learn but we wanted to take the risk and try out the AWC." In addition, the teachers committed to mutual support, collaboration, and acceptance of the inevitable: they would make some mistakes along the way.

The group set up periodic meetings. Most of the work took place online. Group members emailed each other on a semi-regular basis, opening up to their colleagues with everything from good ideas to distressing discoveries. In an interview for the National Writing Project journal, *The Quarterly*, Jeffrey Wilhelm (Devlin, 2003) promoted the idea of online conferencing as a great way to build community:

> I think a lot of times in schools we close our doors, and we kill our own snakes. And we might not have people in our school who we trust, or who can help us . . . and so that's a nice thing about an online community. You have people who may be several states away who are thinking hard about the same things you are, who might be able to offer you an angle or advice. (pp. 8, 21)

For his part, Wilhelm could see that the inquiry projects were well worth publishing. He threw out some deadlines to the group just to up the ante. They were to bring everything they had—all their data—to an April meeting. In July, the group gathered in a rented home in Sun Valley and wrote for days.

Diedrich offers practical advice for others who might want to start a teacher research project:

- Teachers are the busiest people. You can't wait for the perfect day to get together. Set dates ahead of time. Be prepared to meet on weekends.
- Classroom inquiry is real work. Each researcher deserves a stipend of some kind.
- Prepare teachers to be flexible. You don't always follow the path you were expecting to go down.
- Set deadlines.
- Stick together. (Remember Diedrich's analogy with quitting smoking. It's not always so easy to do on your own.)
- The leader needs to invite regular communication. Just ask: "What's happening? What's going well? What isn't going so well?"
- Make the meetings efficient. In this case, meetings lasted an hour. They consisted of updates, concerns, issues, shared ideas, plus lots of reassurance. Diedrich advises: "Set the stage for the meetings by reiterating that it's okay if you're not very far along. We're not making comparisons here. No one has to prove anything."

And once the party's over, is there an aftermath? Or did the Boise and Michigan teachers just fade back into their classrooms and plow on with the usual lessons? If Diedrich is any kind of example, the answer goes like this: "The AWC has never left my classroom. I still communicate with teachers from the group. They're my Facebook friends. We're still supporting each other."

One more word about support: It's important that school administrators understand the benefits of an inquiry group. Diedrich explains that her administrators encourage her professional learning because "they know I will come back and share my knowledge with those around me, both in my building and within my district. I have built a positive reputation for myself as a teacher-leader who is always striving to improve my methods so I can help every single one of my students succeed, not just in my classroom, but in life."

The Idaho inquiry project started with one teacher's idea of how to introduce his local colleagues to the AWC. Throughout its existence, the project remained a volunteer, grassroots undertaking. It proceeded without a script or formula, and it lived in harmony with local policy initiatives like the Idaho state writing assessment. In the next section we present other possibilities for introducing the AWC to teacher colleagues. Keep in mind that professional development, like teacher inquiry, does not have to be an elaborate affair. In many cases, the more homegrown, the better, especially in terms of credibility. When teachers learn from one another, they are much more likely to welcome new ideas.

THE AWC IN PROFESSIONAL DEVELOPMENT

When the Writing Project made its debut in 1974, the notion of "teachers teaching teachers" was revolutionary. To founder Jim Gray, the idea meant that experienced teachers would provide their colleagues with *classroom-tested* approaches rather than something a curriculum "expert" made up. Indeed, Gray (2000) viewed teachers as the centerpieces of reform or, as he also referred to them, "the key players" (p. 50). Their practices had weight and volume, having stood up to real students in real classrooms. Thus, teachers could account for the thinking behind a particular technique or tool, its evolution and challenges, and most important, whatever questions and possibilities arose from its use in the classroom.

Working with Elementary Teachers

We begin this section with an example of an elementary teacher who put the AWC to the test in her own "laboratory" before offering it to others. Linda Buchanan, who is also a media specialist, immersed herself in using the AWC with students in Tupelo, Mississippi. There, she and her colleagues, Carol Wright and Kay Collins, developed a kid-friendly version of the AWC and used it to teach revision to their own students. Once they had worked through their lessons and studied the results, they were ready to lead teachers in their school through professional development that would allow these teachers, in turn, to use the AWC for the benefit of their students.

First Step: Developing and Classroom Testing a Writing Activity. Buchanan's series of lessons on informative writing began with students collaboratively researching and writing about an animal. Students read from mentor texts. "What is interesting about this animal? What's funny? What questions do you have?" Buchanan asked her students. Ultimately, students chose one animal for their collaborative writing, giving specific reasons for their choice: "Squirrels do interesting things." "We have a lot of information about squirrels." "I have three in my backyard, but I have never seen inside a nest." A collective first draft emerged.[2]

Focusing first on the CONTENT attribute and then on the others, students revisited their class draft, color-coding for categories of information. The coding revealed gaps. "We have three yellow sentences about how squirrels look and only one brown sentence about what they eat." They returned to mentor texts to close those gaps and also to look for examples of good beginnings and powerful endings to engage readers. Along the way, they learned some important lessons in how to connect ideas. Buchanan later described it this way to colleagues:

> If you have a paragraph about what the animal looks like, you might help the students select one characteristic to lead into the next paragraph about its habitat, for example:
>> Paragraph 1: Squirrels are mostly gray like tree trunks, so their color helps them to hide in trees.
>> Paragraph 2: Squirrels spend most of their time in trees. . . . "

Revising for STANCE came more easily. As Buchanan explained, "I reminded students that they had already been thinking about their audience when they chose details and an opening to draw the reader in."

In fact, revision became a natural daily activity. After each lesson, Buchanan made computer revisions to the class draft and distributed copies to students. As her class moved through processes for SENTENCE FLUENCY, DICTION, and CONVENTIONS, students began to compose individual informational books and revise them, responding to one another's progress.

Second Step: Demonstrating a Classroom-Tested Practice to Teachers. Buchanan routinely takes notes about what works with her students, what doesn't, and what changes in the teaching process seem necessary. By the time she shares the lessons with her colleagues, she can trace her own trial-and-error process as well as give them some tangible takeaways, such as the following:

- An Analytic Scoring Continuum that has been translated into more accessible language for young writers
- A look at the what, why, and how of mentor texts as models of the attributes of good writing. For teachers who are less familiar with mentor texts or who are always looking for new ways to use them, this portion of the professional development session is particularly important:

  > Mentor texts are as comfortable as a worn pair of blue jeans. Their familiarity allows us to concentrate on writing skills and strategies—we know the text well. They ignite the writer's imagination and determination to create high-quality text that mirror the mentor text in many ways. Mentor texts help writers notice things about an author's work that is not like anything they might have done before, and empower them to try something new. (Dorfman & Cappeli, 2007, p. 3)

- Processes for using the AWC to teach revision
- A strategy for teaching students how to shape and connect their ideas

Finally, note the richness of one writing assignment, both in the classroom and as a model for teachers in professional development. Students read and reread the mentor text; they draft and revise collaboratively to prepare for their own writing; and they learn the language of the AWC along the way.

Working with Secondary Teachers

In contrast to the previous example of professional development related to the AWC, this one depends less on a classroom-tested practice and more on introducing the AWC itself as a multipurpose tool—one that gives teachers and students the language and concepts they need to discover strengths and possibilities in a piece of writing on the road to revision. This kind of an introduction is not unlike the unfolding of the AWC in Chapter 2, "The Attributes of Good Writing." Notice, however, that in this context, the AWC becomes a tool for addressing a particular problem, one that has brought the teachers together at this particular time.

The time was right in Mississippi for teachers to beef up their writing lessons. The state writing assessment raised the stakes for everyone—teachers and students alike. Writing project leader Emily Noble, an 18-year veteran in education, got the call to meet on a Saturday with Rankin County secondary teachers who agreed to bring along student work from their classrooms. Their goal was to use the AWC to design revision lessons. Secretly, however, the teachers were hoping for something in the fast-track category, a quick way of preparing for the test.

Noble introduced the AWC to the group. It was instantly clear that this was not a fast-track tool. It took time to unpack, and how were all these words and score points going to add up to better student writing? Noble persisted. The teachers went along with her, impatient as they were for any answer that would result in high scores. Then Noble played her ace card and the group came to life.

"Once I brought out the student writing, the whole thing started to make sense to the teachers. They actually got excited," Noble said.[3] Indeed, someone immediately commented, "I have kids who write just like this." Another teacher observed that she might be paying too much attention to the number of paragraphs in a piece. Still another thought she probably concentrated a bit too heavily on the thesis statement. Clearly, these teachers were able to see right away that the AWC applied to the writing of *their* students.

Because Noble selected papers to represent each score point of the AWC, teachers could also see dramatic differences, for example, when the writing was **very well suited to purpose and audience** (score point 6) compared to writing that was **inappropriate to purpose and audience** (score point 3). And in all cases, teachers came to value CONTENT, or as one teacher put it, "the AWC gives me a new perspective about what's important. I need to craft lessons on content instead of structure."

Then the teacher participants pulled out their own students' work. The writing—viewed through the AWC lens—revealed that students lacked audience awareness. "For too long our kids have written to the teacher," noted one participant. Working with partners, the teachers practiced diagnosing various pieces of writing and then rehearsed how they would respond to the students, using the language of the AWC. Noble also provided model lessons on response and revision—showing how lessons might look when the AWC provides the language and direction.

Noble sees particular value in the practice/rehearsal phase of the session. "I want teachers to get past our traditional ways of talking to students about their writing. A good starting place for a conversation is to note that a paper would benefit from more details. And then, teachers can help students look for relevant details by saying, 'Right here where you talked about your fishing trip, you said you had a lot of fun—what did that look like?'" This kind of comment reflects a deeper understanding of content, audience and purpose.

What made this professional development effort successful was the way in which the teachers participated, for instance, coming with a specific purpose, looking at sample papers, practicing with other teachers, and being part of planned follow-up discussions. But the biggest takeaway is that teachers applied the AWC to the writing that mattered to them—writing that came straight from their students and that would go back to those students. In other words, the design of this professional development ensured that the participants had more than a tool in their backpacks or tote bags when they left for home—they had a start on putting the tool to work in their classrooms.

SETTING UP PROFESSIONAL DEVELOPMENT IN YOUR BACKYARD

We devote the next section to more possibilities for using the AWC in professional development sessions and for expanding the kinds of writing to use with the AWC. For starters, everyone seems to agree that examining student work is productive and enlightening and is a surefire way to learn what's happening. However, many teachers we know have participated in professional development sessions to which they brought papers to "look at," but no one seemed to know what to do with them. Is there a productive way to focus the talk about student writing?

Several years ago, Mary Ann begged her way into a 7:00 A.M. professional development session with a dozen veterinarians—half new to the profession and half experienced—to see how dog and cat doctors study their cases. After a scramble for coffee, the group focused its attention on a young woman, who was a novice vet, and an x-ray of a cat she popped into a light box on the wall. She selected this case because it presented a problem, one that merited the help of her colleagues. The cat had an abscessed tooth. The owner wanted an immediate extraction, but as the novice vet pointed out on the x-ray, the cat also had an enlarged heart. Would surgery be dangerous, she wanted to know?

The doctors didn't rush to answer her question. Rather, they asked her questions. For example, how had she handled the situation so far? Only after she reached the end of her practical knowledge did they offer their suggestions: "You have to take care of the heart failure first. Treat for the treatable right now" (Smith, 2003, p. 19).

When she first wrote about this scenario, Mary Ann noted the parallels with professional development in her own field:

> I imagine a piece of student writing in place of the shadowy cat. Surrounded by supportive colleagues, a teacher presents the case: brief background on the student and brief description of the events and intentions that led to this piece of writing. Then, a collective look at the student work. At any point in my teaching career, I would have leaped at the chance to unravel a tangled piece of writing in the company of peers. (Smith, 2003, p. 19)

Studying writing case-by-case, using the AWC, is another worthy professional development strategy. So let's pop a piece of writing in the light box and see how it works. First, Missouri teacher Julie Sheerman tells us this about the student:

> Cory is a bright student who doesn't think of himself a writer. He juggles many demands on his time, including sports, a part-time job, and a difficult course load. Cory produced this work early in his senior year. At the time, he wrote mainly to finish assignments.[4]

To introduce Cory's piece of writing, Sheerman says it was written to the prompt "What is success for you?" Then she notes that it is "list like" and asks other teachers for their suggestions, just as the young vet asked her colleagues for suggestions:

> I want to ask my colleagues to tell me what they see as the strengths of this writing and then talk about how to develop the generalizations like "community," "success," "enjoyment." The ideas in the writing need more concrete details. Would my colleagues agree with this?

Now read Cory's paper (excerpted here) and think about where Sheerman asks us to concentrate our response:

> My terms of success might be very different from others. I do not care about the amount of money I make, or the size of the house that I live

in. I could care less about having fancy things and luxury Items. I care about making a decent living and being able to keep food on the table for my family and I. I want to live comfortably and be respected by everybody around me, as I will respect them as well.

To be successful in highschool I want to maintain a 4.0 grade average and be active in the school and my community. My terms of success aren't being an all star on the football field, or the smartest kid in school, but trying my best in each and everything that I do. I want to have many friends and enjoy spending time with them every single day while I am in highschool. I think being successful in high school is all about trying hard at school and enjoying the time you have with your friends and family.

Keep in mind here that Sheerman uses the AWC in her teaching of writing. For this case of student writing, our feedback in the language of the AWC will be most helpful. The strength of this writing is its **focus**. It contains **ideas that sometimes support the topic** of success. For example, for Cory, success in life is "making a decent living" and being "respected by everybody"; it is not "the size of the house I live in" or "having fancy things." Ideas in the next paragraph relate to his definition of success in high school: a "4.0 grade average," "trying my best," "having many friends," and "enjoying the time you have with your friends." In short, the ideas are **purposeful**.

Sheerman has also asked if we see what she sees in this writing in terms of problems, just as the young vet asked her colleagues if they agreed with her diagnosis of the cat's health issues. We do, right? We want this writing to flesh out the abstractions with more details, more examples, and more development. That would be the next step for Cory. What does he mean by things like "decent living" and "live comfortably?"

Looking at an example of student writing like this one can be the entire focus of a professional development session because the discussion branches out to what teachers can do to help students build more content or better organization. What strategies work best? The writing is the touchstone, the AWC supplies the attributes and language, and the teachers—like the veterinarians—bring the classroom experience.

And just to let you know what happened to Cory during his senior year in Sheerman's English class, here is a brief summary from his teacher:

Because of the time we spend routinely free writing in class, his fluency grew over the year. In time, Cory wrote to express his feelings and explore his own thoughts. While this piece seems list-like, Cory ended strong. I think his writing grew with some instruction and practice, improving greatly in the areas of content and sentence fluency. Prior to grade 12, he viewed sentences as correct or incorrect. Of my students, Cory demonstrated the greatest interest in play and experimentation.

Through sentence revision, he grew as a writer. The initial mechanical changes to his sentences led to Cory exploring ideas more deeply and in original ways.

CONNECTING THE AWC TO PREPARING FOR COLLEGE AND CAREER

For professional development programs centered on particular standards, for example the Common Core, the AWC may be useful as a guide—whether for scoring or talking together about student writing samples. Part of that process might be to line up the AWC with CCSS descriptions of college and career readiness.

Lining Up the AWC with College and Career Readiness

The Common Core State Standards for English Language Arts and Literacy in History/Social Studies, Science, and Technical Subjects offer a "portrait of students who meet the standards set out in this document." Here are three of the main descriptors of what college-ready students do:

They build strong content knowledge.

Students establish a base of knowledge across a wide range of subject matter by engaging with works of quality and substance. They become proficient in new areas through research and study. They read purposefully and listen attentively to gain both general knowledge and discipline-specific expertise. They refine and share their knowledge through writing and speaking.

They respond to the varying demands of audience, task, purpose, and discipline.

Students adapt their communication in relation to audience, task, purpose, and discipline. They set and adjust purpose for reading, writing, speaking, listening, and language use as warranted by the task. They appreciate nuances, such as how the composition of an audience should affect tone when speaking and how the connotations of words affect meaning. They also know that different disciplines call for different types of evidence (e.g., documentary evidence in history, experimental evidence in science).

They value evidence.

Students cite specific evidence when offering an oral or written interpretation of a text. They use relevant evidence when supporting their own points in writing and speaking, making their reasoning clear to the reader or listener, and they constructively evaluate others' use of evidence. (CCSSO & NGA, 2010, p. 7)

The AWC attributes of good writing correspond with what college-ready students are expected to do: collect and use strong CONTENT in their writing; attend to **audience and purpose;** address the audience in the appropriate **tone;** pay attention to DICTION; and, not to be forgotten, fall in love with **evidence** and cite it specifically.

Lining up the AWC with Professional Writing

Mentor texts are as important in professional development as they are in the classroom. Teachers benefit from sharing strategies for using mentor texts and from knowing in what ways they help students:

> If I want my students to write editorials, it helps to show them some strong editorials. If I want my students to write reviews for Amazon.com, we spend some time looking at some previously posted Amazon reviews. Yes, it is important to show students how the teacher writes, but it is also of paramount importance to provide students with mentor texts so they can see how other writers compose. It is critical that my students be able to move beyond simply telling me what a text says; I want them to begin to recognize how the text is constructed. I certainly want them to stand next to me while I write, but I also want them to stand next to Anna Quindlen, or Rick Reilly, or Leonard Pitts and notice what they do when they write. I want them to see how they write. (Gallagher, 2011, p. 20)

Because the AWC is a tool for looking at how a text works, it is ideal for mentor texts such as the following by Jonathan Freedland, a British journalist who writes a weekly column for *The Guardian* and a monthly piece for the *Jewish Chronicle*. In his piece, "The Selfie's Screaming Narcissism Masks an Urge to Connect," Freedland delves into the popularity of the selfie and what lurks behind this craze, and in the process features the attributes of good writing:

> The Oxford Dictionaries' word of the year, "selfie," seems to be all about me, me, me. But its social nature reveals a desperate search for an us.
>
> What greater testament could there be to the "me generation" than the rise and rise of the selfie? Anointed by Oxford Dictionaries' editors as the word of the year after a 17,000% increase in its usage, the selfie is surely the ultimate emblem of the age of narcissism. Like the doomed figure of ancient myth, we cannot stop gazing at our own reflection. This July, there were an estimated 90M photos on Instagram—the go-to platform for the selfie—with the hashtag #me. And that figure will be far, far higher now.

At first glance, everything about this phenomenon reeks. It is self-centered in the most literal sense. Not for nothing is the word just a breath—a mere "sh"—away from selfish.

What's more, it's selfishness of the most superficial kind. It's not just about me, me, me but how I look, look, look. It invites judgment based on appearance alone. You post a picture of yourself and wait for the verdict, your self-worth boosted by a happy spate of "likes," or destroyed by the opposite—a resounding silence. At least on Twitter, people are judgmental about each other's wit or ideas, rather than their hair.

To understand the sheer scale—the depth, if you like—of this superficiality, look no further than this Tumblr dedicated to selfies at funerals, including the image captioned: "Love my hair today. Hate why I'm dressed up #funeral."

And yet condemnation cannot be the only response to a phenomenon this widespread, which clearly delights so many tens of millions. The informality of the word "selfie" suggests something true about these instant self-portraits: that they don't take themselves or their subjects too seriously. To quote the artist Gillian Wearing: "The word 'selfie' is brilliant. It really encapsulates a time: instant, quick, funny. It sounds ironic and throwaway."

It is also true that, while the technology may be new, the instinct it satisfies is not: since the dawn of civilisation, humans have yearned to depict themselves and their faces—whether through cave paint, clay or, today, the megapixels of a smartphone.

Above all, and this might be the selfie's redeeming feature, they are not designed to be looked at solely by the subject. The selfie's usual purpose is to be transmitted by social media—with "social" being the key word. They may be focused on the self, but they also express a timeless human need to connect with others.

In that respect, the selfie is like so much else in the digital world—all about "me," but revealing a sometimes desperate urge to find an "us." (Freedland, 2013)

Clearly, Freedland writes for an audience that understands and/or uses social media and selfies in particular. While he mocks the "me, me, me" nature of selfies—so easy to dismiss as self-serving—he refuses to settle for the obvious. Rather, he proposes the idea that human beings have social cravings and historic urges to connect with others.

Now what happens if we take the first three attributes of the AWC (CONTENT, STRUCTURE, STANCE) and view the piece alongside them. In what ways does the AWC pick up its characteristics?

Content: The writing is **clear and consistently focused** on the idea of the selfie. It exhibits **outstanding control and development,** examining several ways of looking at the selfie with **ideas that are consistently purposeful and specific.** It contains **evidence** that the selfie is a growing phenomenon with roots in human history, and it provides several sources of evidence to back up assertions.

Structure: The writing is organized so that it **enhances the central idea,** including a provocative question to open and a **sense of resolution** (and hope!) to close. **Smooth and cohesive transitions** connect ideas and move from the more obvious reasons for selfies to a more nuanced possibility.

Stance: The writing aims at a general audience and, in particular, one that understands or uses social media and selfies. The purpose is a critical exploration of why the selfie has shot through the roof in popularity and what that means. There is a **clear perspective** summed up in the conclusion: the selfie is more than it appears to be. The **level of formality is very well suited for the purpose and audience.**

Looking at the attributes in a professional piece of writing gives teachers and ultimately their students new ideas about how to write openings or move to an alternate point of view or weave in evidence. For example, Freedman manages to consider the selfie through social, historical, and psychological lenses, something students might not have considered before examining his essay.

Lining Up the AWC with Teacher Writing

Another key activity in a professional development workshop is for teachers to try out creating their own piece of writing, something that helps them understand more about the teaching of writing. In this case, after reading the Friedman piece, teachers might write about a trend or current phenomenon, in much the way Freedman explored the selfie, trying to account for it from multiple points of view. Another alternative is for teachers to write about a personal or family passion, not in terms of its chronological development, but in terms of its attractiveness, both the obvious and less obvious. With either topic, teachers experience firsthand how a writer makes use of a mentor text. In subsequent discussions, they can share how to help students in the same endeavor. Teachers can also look at their own writing through the lens of the AWC, perhaps focusing on one attribute that interests them. Again, the firsthand experience will translate into more informed teaching in the classroom.

There are many reasons why teachers should write themselves:

- They become better teachers. "The best writing teachers are writers themselves. Why? Because we know the writing process inside out, we can support our students' work in authentic ways." (O'Donnell-Allen, 2012, para 11)

- They learn about what it takes to draft and revise. Looking back at teachers who wrote in the Bay Area Writing Project summer institutes, James Gray (2000) noted:

  > They rise to a new level; when they leave the institute they're teachers of writing *who are also writers* . . . We'd get comments like, "I always thought I knew what revision meant until this summer. *Now* I know what revision means!" and, "I've learned more about the teaching of writing than I've ever known before, and I learned most through the writing I did." (p. 85)

- Students often have the impression that teachers are gifted writers who never struggle for words or ideas. Rebecca Alber (2012) says that watching teachers write gives students the "invaluable message":

  > I struggle too. I get tongue-tied and run out of things to say. I repeat myself and I forget words that I know I've used in the past. I sometimes change my mind halfway through a page, or even two, and want to start over with a new topic. Writing isn't always so easy! (para 6)

- Teacher writing is another model for students—both process and product—and this model can be live and in real time.

So we advocate for teachers to write during professional development workshops, to try out whatever strategy or assignment is under consideration, and to learn more about their writing by consulting the AWC.

The reason to try out the AWC with our own writing is not to get a score, but to see how the attributes show up in our personal or professional efforts. In fact, teachers have done this very thing with interesting results. Mississippi writing teacher Kim Patterson Roberts, in particular, credits the AWC with taking her writing beyond the chaos stage:

> We all know writing is messy and it's complex, so it's not something that you can go in and say "we're going to do this" and it's not like a mathematical formula. But I think that the continuum helps me organize that complexity and chaos that is often writing. And I know it helps me as a writer. When I sit down to write something and I typically just write, write, write, just blah on the page to begin with. But when I go in to look at it again, to do some revision, I don't pull the rubric out necessarily, pull that continuum out, but I often think about okay, let's think, do each of my sentences flow nicely into one another? I really internalize those characteristics.
>
> I can look at a piece of my own writing or look at a piece of writing of others and just kind of almost naturally tick through those characteristics and think about where I see those in the paper and so in

some ways, it organizes my thinking around a piece of writing. It's not just—there is a certain amount of kind of magic that happens when the pen gets to flowing, because writing is so complex. But that continuum really does kind of lend a method to the madness. (personal communication, June 20, 2008)

YOUR TURN

The big message in this chapter is pretty straightforward: Play around with the AWC enough that you are comfortable with it, whether on your own or with a teacher group. Put the AWC next to your students' writing, your own writing, your choice of mentor texts, and go from there. Your experience will no doubt enrich the use of the AWC beyond what we have imagined. And then don't hesitate to share with your colleagues, whether formally or informally. As Linda Buchanan demonstrated, your trial-and-error efforts with the AWC in your classroom bring a much-needed resource to other teachers.

CHAPTER 5

Setting Up a Local Scoring Session

Throughout this book we have referred to large NWP national scorings with student papers from around the country. In this section, we are going local, where scorings may take place in a school, district, or writing project site with writing from a certain group of students (for example, one grade level or a cluster of grade levels) or writing of a certain kind (for example, one subject area or one genre of writing). The purpose for the scoring is also a local matter, because scoring papers is a way to get information for planning, creating curriculum, assessing current programs, and communicating with parents. It is also a way to establish a professional community of teachers. Goals like these are positive and productive because they are meant to help students with their writing. Such goals ensure that whether or not the students ultimately know how they scored during a local assessment, they will not suffer any ill effects. Instead, scoring with a tool like the AWC gives local educators a basis for decisions about what's next, what's best, what counts. This does not mean that scoring with the AWC is limited to "low-stakes" situations. But for our discussion, we will keep our focus on doable, informative scoring efforts by providing ideas for how to set a local scoring session in motion.

THE FIRST STEP: BECOMING FAMILIAR WITH THE SCORING ESSENTIALS

1. The AWC: The first bit of work in any scoring is to become familiar with the scoring guide. While this step sounds logical and, of course, essential—after all, everyone involved has to know the criteria—any introduction to a new way of looking at writing is not a slam dunk. The idea of a scoring guide is to ensure that scorers will apply standards consistently and in alignment with the guide. For the duration of the scoring, teacher scorers, in particular, have to put aside their own ideas about what makes a good piece of writing and agree to follow the rubric. We will give you some tips below for acquainting scorers with the AWC.

2. Anchor papers: Assessing writing requires anchor papers to help interpret the AWC; they are like road maps that keep readers from misinterpreting the scoring guide, thus taking a wrong turn. Anchor papers are demonstrations of score points. They clarify the difference between the 6 paper that is **consistently focused; exceptionally well-shaped and connected** and the 5 paper that is **clear and focused; well-shaped and connected.**

But there is another reason for using anchor papers. As we have noted, teachers are not blank slates. They have their own ideas, standards, and experiences with interpreting and evaluating student writing. When they roll up to a scoring session, they bring it all with them. Suddenly they have to put aside what they have come to believe in order to embrace a different system, a new way of thinking about writing, and a requirement to score according to specific directions. Not easy to do, even temporarily. Anchor papers, combined with the AWC, are their touchstones. Without these, teacher scores could be all over the map.

3. Commentary: When teachers respond to student papers in their own classrooms, they often scrawl comments like "add details" or "explain" or "give evidence." Usually, these comments are prescriptive. They serve as a call to action: "Hey, young writer, you have more work to do."

Commentary in connection with the AWC has a different purpose. It establishes a connection between the AWC and the anchor papers. It explains how a piece of writing fits at a particular score point. In other words, the commentary seals the deal. It says, "This is *why* the score is a 6 or a 5 or a 4."

4. Calibration: Calibration is the process for helping scorers use the scoring criteria to agree on the score for each paper. It involves understanding the scoring guide and trying it out with the anchor papers and commentary. The goal is to ensure that scorers interpret and apply the rubric in the same way. Discussion is a big part of the calibration process. Scorers need to ask questions, to clarify terms, and to come to consensus about how and why the anchor papers represent the score points. Calibration takes place at the beginning of a scoring session, when it is often called "anchoring." It also occurs at intervals throughout as a way to remind scorers about the standards and how they apply to the writing at hand. For those intervals, there are one or more sets of practice papers beyond the anchor set.

THE SECOND STEP: SELECTING LEADERS

1. Chief Reader or Room Leader: These are fancy titles for the person who runs the scoring session and prepares the table leaders and ultimately the scorers. This person is responsible for introducing the AWC, directing the calibration/anchoring procedure, and managing the flow of papers. In a small scoring, the chief reader or room leader sometimes does all the preparation, for example, selecting the anchors and writing commentary. Ideally, more than one person, for example, a committee of teachers, will join in the preparation process.

2. Table Leaders: If the scoring is large enough and there are several tables of scorers, each table should have a leader to help with the training, to work with individual scorers on challenging papers, and to read some of the papers as they are scored, making sure that all scorers are on track.

THE THIRD STEP: SELECTING ANCHORS

Before readers come together to begin scoring, the scoring leaders (chief reader, table leaders, and/or committee members) meet for a day or two to read through a relatively large number of student papers (for example, several full sets of papers from all classes of the chosen grade or several sets of a particular kind of writing). From these papers, they select the anchor papers and write the commentaries for each anchor. In the process, these leaders come to consensus about the standards for each attribute so they can successfully help the scorers reach the same consensus. It's important that everyone has a copy of the AWC. Here are some more detailed suggestions:

What You'll Do: Have your teacher committee and table leaders, plus the chief reader or room leader, begin to read the papers.

- Stop occasionally to pull a few papers from the pile and read them orally. Talk about whether they seem to be high, middle, or low overall and begin three stacks. Continue to read and stack, stopping to read aloud occasionally, especially papers in the high and low categories—and of course to share delights.
- When the stacks each contain a fair number of papers, conduct a finer sort, separating the low category into low-low and high-low; the middle into low-middle and high-middle; and the high category in the same way. Typically, the smallest stack will be the high-high category.
- Using the AWC, read through the papers, matching features of the paper with descriptors. This is a good time to make and attach notes to the papers to help with the final selection of anchors, for example, "4 in content, may be higher in stance" or "6 in content, but low in conventions."
- Make separate stacks of those papers that seem to be "solid" scores, that is, all or almost all the attributes seem to fall on the same score point. It's important for anchors to represent, as far as possible, the same score point for each attribute.

- Keep additional stacks of papers that seem to be "mixed" scores; you may need these as practice papers for calibration. Practice papers also need to be pre-scored and accompanied with commentary.

THE FOURTH STEP: WRITING COMMENTARIES

After selecting the anchors, the next step in the preparation process is writing commentary for each anchor. We suggest that those who are involved in preparation work together on the commentary to build confidence, expertise, and a shared understanding—and, of course, to make the process more enjoyable. Remember that the commentary that goes with each of the anchors and practice papers shines a spotlight on the features of the writing and the corresponding attributes in the AWC. In other words, commentary is a training tool for those who will have to put scores on papers.

Commentary addresses each attribute, one by one. Commentaries are only necessary for the anchor and practice papers, and they are always a bit longer with a 6 paper. In the third-grade example below, the commentary includes quotations from the AWC and cites the paper itself, illustrating the connections between the two and providing evidence for the scores.

Student Writing

I had just left dance, though I hadn't really danced. I pouted in the hallway. "What can I do to get you to try it?" Mom asked. Nothing. So I sat in my bedroom being punished.

"Sadie, come here, quick!" my dad called.

"What?" I moaned. I followed him out to our little playhouse. There, a tiny orange kitten crept.

"Oh my gosh," I said. "He's so cute! Let me hold him!"

"There's another kitten inside," my mom said, showing me a mix-colored kitten. "You can hold them both if you promise to TRY your dance class."

I did NOT want to dance. The tights are annoying and I hate putting my hair in a bun, but I would promise anything to play with those scruffy kitties.

"Can we keep them?"

We sneaked the kittens into the house, building forts for them with blankets and pillows. One went to sleep between two pillows. So cute! To snuggle with them, we trapped them on the couch with stuffed animals and books.

For days the kittens and their mama lived in the playhouse. We used a paint bucket to block the door, but the kittens peeked over it, and then they jumped over it, peeling their bodies through the playhouse door. They sat on the little porch meowing their little meows and tilting their little heads.

One day, we couldn't find them anywhere. We think they grew stronger and went home. I miss them, but I kept my promise.

In dance class, with those kittens on my mind, I didn't worry about my tights or my hair. Now I actually LIKE dance! I am happy that the kittens found their way home.

Or found US on their way home.

The Commentary

- CONTENT 6: The paper reflects **outstanding control and development of consistently purposeful, creative ideas,**, combining details of joyful play with kittens as motivation for enduring the drudgery of dance class. Fully developed details of play with kittens ("holding them both," "sneaked them into the house," "building forts," "peeling their bodies," "tilting their little heads") are juxtaposed beside the unappealing dance class ("tights are annoying," "hair in a bun").

- STRUCTURE 6: The **organization enhances the central idea** of not liking dance but being motivated to try it with the promise of play with kittens. The **compelling opening** establishes the narrator's dislike of dance while the **closing provides an outstanding sense of resolution** that includes appreciation for both dance and the kittens ("Now I actually LIKE dance," "happy that the kittens found their way home. Or found US on their way"). Transitions are smooth and cohesive (For days, in dance class, with those kittens on my mind).

- STANCE 6: The writing **consistently demonstrates a clear perspective through distinctive and sophisticated tone and style,** including the use of dialogue ("Sadie, come here, quick," "What," I moaned). Short sentences accentuate the narrator's distaste for dance ("I pouted in the hallway." "Nothing.") Repetition of words adds stylistic effect (meowing their <u>little</u> meows and tilting their <u>little</u> heads). Precise verbs add to the tone ("crept," "sneaked," "building," "trapped," "block the door," "peeked," "peeling").

- SENTENCE FLUENCY 6: The writing demonstrates **a sophisticated rhythm with very effective phrasing so that each sentence flows into the next.** ("The tights are annoying and I hate putting my hair in a bun, but. . .") **Fragments are deliberately chosen for a stylistic purpose** ("Nothing." "So cute!"). Longer sentences are also deliberate, adding to the cadence and flow of the writing ("We sneaked the kittens into the house, building forts for them with blankets and pillows. . . .").

- DICTION 6: The writing **contains words and expressions that are consistently powerful, precise, creative, and yet natural** ("sat in my bedroom being punished," "mix-colored kitten," "scruffy kittens,"

"trapped them on the couch"). The writing contains **lively verbs**
("pouted," "moaned," "crept," "snuggle," "block," "peeked"), **precise nouns** ("paint bucket"), and **imagery** ("peeling their bodies").
- CONVENTIONS 6: The writing is **almost error-free and demonstrates
  outstanding control of age-appropriate standard writing conventions** (internal commas, dialogue). **Almost no editing is needed.**

To illustrate further, here is an example of a secondary problem–solution paper at the lower end of the scale and some initial work toward commentary.

Student Writing

About 40,600 wild horses roam lands in 10 Western states. The population has gotten so big that the land can't support the horses with
enough food. The U.S. Bureau of Land Management should help the
horses by picking up so many from each state take them in to a shelter,
break them, then put them up for adoption.

   If they did this it would help everyone out. It would make enough
room on each land for the horse to have enough to eat and also people at the shelters will have a great time with horses. You can't forget
about how many smiles you will see from childrens to adults that are
horse lovers.

The Commentary

- CONTENT 3: The writing presents a **discernable focus** that the horses
  should be picked up, put in a shelter, and put up for adoption. The
  paper rises above a score of 2 in that the **ideas somewhat support
  the central topic but are usually poorly developed.**
- STRUCTURE 3: The writing presents an **organization that is minimally adequate** for developing a problem and solution. The opening
  sets up the problem but the piece loses steam in the second paragraph when the closing does not manage to tie the piece together.
- STANCE 3: THe facts regarding the number of horses and the subsequent lack of sufficient food suggest a stance of advocacy for the
  horses. However, the **tone becomes uneven and the style sporadic**
  when the writing jumps from the Bureau of Land Management to
  smiling children and adults at the shelters.
- SENTENCE FLUENCY 3: The writing exhibits a variety of sentence
  structures and lengths, yet the **relationships among ideas are only
  somewhat established.** For example: "The population has gotten so
  big that the land can't support the horses with enough food. . . If
  they did this it would help everyone out . . . it would make enough
  room on each land. . . ."

- DICTION 2: The piece contains language that **is occasionally clear and precise**, yet contains **some vague words that are confusing** ("So many from each state," "room on each land, if they did this," "people at the shelters")
- CONVENTIONS 3: The writing exhibits some errors in internal punctuation but demonstrates **reasonable control over a limited range of age-appropriate standard writing conventions** (e.g., initial capitals, end punctuation).

Note first that the commentary is shorter on a lower-scoring paper. However, it still cites strengths even as it identifies weaknesses. In other words, there is a discernable pattern in these commentaries—find the good stuff first. Also note that not every attribute in this piece earns a score point of 3. DICTION, because of the vague expressions, earns a score of 2. As you may recall, this is one of the advantages of analytic scoring. It allows scorers to distinguish among the attributes, giving separate scores for each. A holistic score does not provide information about individual attributes and thus is not as useful for making teaching decisions based on the assessment.

INTRODUCING THE AWC TO SCORERS

When the big moment arrives and scorers are in place, the first task is to help everyone understand and commit to the AWC as the standard for the scoring. We offer some fairly detailed steps below, with the caveat that this procedure is not the only way to go. However, it is the process that room leaders and table leaders use at NWP national scorings, so we are confident that it has been thoroughly tested.

Begin with the CONTENT Attribute

- Read all the bullets under score point 6 to get an overall picture of superior content. Notice there are four bullets or threads that describe the content attribute.
- Read the first bullet or thread under score point 6; now look at the first thread under score point 5, now 4, now 3, and across to 1. What is the thread about? What aspect of content does it address? Find a key word that describes this aspect. Teachers usually say "focus."
- Write that word beside that first bullet or thread.
- Now look again at the first bullet at score point 6. What's the difference between a score of 6 and a score of 5 for that bullet or thread? Underline and read aloud the qualifying words. The qualifying words are the key to where a piece of writing will fall on

Figure 5.1. Identifying a Key Word for Each Thread and Highlighting Qualifying Words

	6. The writing:	5. The writing:	4. The writing:
	» Is *clear and consistently* focused; *exceptionally* well shaped and connected.	» Is *clear* and focused; *well shaped* and connected.	» Is *generally clear* and focused; *satisfactorily shaped* and connected.
Focus	3. The writing:	2. The writing:	1. The writing:
	» Has a *discernible* focus; *sometimes shaped* and connected.	» May present several ideas, but *no central focus* emerges; *seldom shaped* and connected.	» May announce the topic, but *no central focus is present; not at all shaped* and connected.

the continuum, so you want to emphasize how these descriptors change, or even disappear, at each score point. Figure 5.1 illustrates how a key word captures the gist of the thread, and how highlighting the qualifiers—which distinguish one score point from another—draws extra attention to them.

Continue the Process

- Read the second bullet or thread under each score point, starting with the 6 and continuing across to the 1. Determine the subject of that bullet or thread. Some teachers refer to this thread as "control and development." This one is pretty obvious, isn't it?
- Now look again at the second bullet or thread under score point 6. What's the difference between a score of 6 and a score of 5 for that thread? Underline and read aloud the qualifying words. Again, the emphasis is on the qualifying words, which signal where on the continuum a piece of writing will fit most comfortably.
- Ask yourself, how do the descriptors change from a 5 to a 4, from a 4 to a 3, and so on to the 2 and the 1?
- Continue for each bullet, first naming it and then underlining and reading aloud the qualifying words across the score points. (Note that at the lower score points, a bullet will occasionally disappear or be combined with another.)
- Check for shared understanding of language.
- Continue through all the attributes, studying and labeling the bullets or threads, determining how each score point differs from adjacent scores, and highlighting the qualifiying words. Figure

Figure 5.2. Identifying Key Words and Highlighting Qualifiers

	6. The writing:	5. The writing:	4. The writing:
Control and Development	» Reflects *outstanding control* and development of ideas and content.	» Reflects *strong control* and development of ideas and content.	» Reflects *good control* and development of ideas and content.
	3. The writing:	2. The writing:	1. The writing:
	» Reflects *limited control* and development of ideas and content.	» Reflects *little control* or development of ideas and content.	» Reflects *minimal or no control* of ideas and content.

5.2 provides another illustration of using a key word to name the essence of the thread or bullet and then giving prominence to the all-important qualifiers.

Working methodically through the AWC builds an understanding of the common lens, language, set of standards, and nuanced differences that separate one score point from another. The next steps are to look at the AWC alongside the anchor papers and the commentary. In a national scoring, this whole process takes several hours. The papers anchor or moor the AWC to an actual performance; they show what **clear and consistently focused** actually looks like as compared to **generally clear and focused**. And, of course, the commentary completes the picture by combining language from the paper and the AWC.

You might not come to the conclusion, after reading all these directions, that scoring student papers is interesting and engaging. However, it's not at all the same as sitting by yourself late at night trying to grade and comment on several weeks' worth of assignments. At a scoring session you are with friends and colleagues. You find yourself taking notes on their observations. If you're lucky, there are food and adequate breaks. (Actually, these last items are essential.) We promise that you will laugh at least once in a while, and, for sure, you will learn a lot about examining writing and teaching writers.

CHAPTER 6

The Power and Potential of Invention

"Teaching writing is all about invention," claims Michigan teacher Paula Diedrich. "And of course, I pass along to my students the power to invent." You may remember Diedrich as the teacher leader of the AWC action research project (see Chapter 4). As a teacher of eighth grade students, she encourages their ideas at every turn. "Why would I want to read the same 112 research papers?" she asks. "I want the kids to write about what interests them."[1]

For Diedrich and so many other teachers, invention is "one reason we love our jobs in spite of the pressures." When Diedrich first encountered the AWC, she wanted others to have it. "Invention is also about figuring out ways to share and to make life easier for other people. Ben Franklin didn't invent bifocals just so *he* could see better."

In this chapter, we offer some ideas for getting started with the Analytic Writing Continuum, and we encourage our readers to invent more ways to use it for improving your students' writing.

BRINGING THE AWC TO YOUR CLASSROOM

The ideas below originated with the teachers featured in previous chapters and others who experimented with the AWC and then shared those experiments. What these teachers have in common is the desire to be as specific and helpful as possible when they tell their students how to make their writing better. They also want to teach writing in such a way that they see improvement where their students are concerned. Most teachers know how frustrating it is when students seem to be stuck, when there are no visible gains.

Here are several things to keep in mind when starting out with the AWC. It's not a document that will have much meaning to students without you. In other words, you can't just pass it out in class or assign it for homework. And that really is the good news. We've had enough of materials that eliminate teachers. You have the absolute authority to make this rubric work for your situation. As each of our classroom stories illustrate (see Chapter 3), when the AWC made its debut, the teacher had a purpose in mind and a way to introduce it to a particular group of students.

Another reminder: The AWC also lacks much meaning in the absence of student writing. However you pave the way for your students, you will want to have some writing close at hand so you can point to things like outstanding control and development of ideas or smooth transitions or formality that is well-suited for purpose and audience. The AWC lends itself best to showing, not telling.

This seems a good time to reiterate one more of our themes. The AWC is most effective when teachers and students approach it together, and for the optimum conditions, when teachers collaborate with other teachers. If you have a special colleague or colleagues who might jump into a new endeavor, sign them on. The teachers whose stories show up in this book were not flying solo. They joined a professional community that supported their everyday inventions and successes, and conversely, that eased their doubts and disappointments on less-than-good days.

And finally, think about easing the AWC into your teaching. We all know how cumbersome it is when some innovation comes along and suddenly we have to start shoving everything else out of the way to make room for it. The AWC is a tool that actually makes an already time-consuming part of the curriculum—teaching writing—more manageable. Here are some one-step-at-a-time possibilities:

- *Begin with one attribute.* If you read articles about the benefits of exercise (which seem to be everywhere these days), you know that the experts try to coax you into getting started by saying things like "just begin by walking 10 minutes a day." The same advice applies here. Select one attribute that makes the most sense as a place to take off. Dehoney (see Chapter 3) pulled out the CONTENT attribute first for her second graders. Mumm actually started with two—SENTENCE FLUENCY and DICTION—with her EL students in mind. While CONTENT is typically the building block, there is no lockstep order, as the Mumm example illustrates.
- *Use real student writing samples.* Start with one. Start with ten minutes a day like the exercise guru recommends. However you take the plunge, showing how one or more attributes work with a piece of writing is the ticket here. And here's what you might expect: Students are always interested in what other kids are writing, so using student samples (with the writer unidentified) provides the ideal situation for introducing the AWC lens and language.
- *Use professional writing/mentor texts.* Whatever you are reading in class may be just right for an analysis with the AWC. As Gallagher (2011) reminds us, " . . . we must move our writing instruction beyond a 'cover the standards' mind-set by introducing our young writers to additional real-world discourses . . ." (p. 8). We have

made several arguments for using mentor texts in combination with the AWC. When we show students that the AWC works just as well with their own writing as it does with professional writing, they may give it a little extra attention and respect. For maximum effect, try using the AWC with your writing.

- **Have students score papers.** We have heartily endorsed this idea before, but here is another argument in favor of students learning to assess their own work: Edward White (2007) notes that students do not revise their work because "they don't really think there is anything wrong with it" (p. 84). This is at heart an assessment problem. If students could learn to assess their own work, they would be much more likely to adopt the work habits of professional writers—who usually consider the first draft as working copy to get them started, not the end of the line (p. 84).

  One engaging way for students to learn self-assessment is to participate in a scoring—a highly social activity that involves understanding and applying the attributes, making judgments, and debriefing. Again, you want the papers to be anonymous and the conversation focused on the AWC. Students can score individually, in partners, or in small groups.

- **Use the AWC for minilessons.** Short, sharply focused lessons on writing attributes—for example, embedding anecdotes (CONTENT), crafting compelling openings (STRUCTURE), establishing tone (STANCE), varying sentence structures (SENTENCE FLUENCY), using lively verbs (DICTION), or working with capitalization (CONVENTIONS)—help students learn *how* to put the attributes to work in their own writing. NWP leaders used minilessons at the national scoring sessions to teach the scorers about the attribute STANCE by visually representing different perspectives or ways of looking at a subject.

- **Create and post class lists or keep writing notebooks.** For the AWC to be effective as a teaching tool, it needs the power of practice and repetition. You can help students collect and remember all those minilessons in lists and notebooks. Lists might also include ideas for developing content, ideas for making things clear, and different ways to handle organization.

- **Use the AWC to create other rubrics.** The AWC is open to revision. If it needs to be more friendly for younger students, then go for it. Make the language suitable for the students in your class or classes. However, it's a good idea when you revise the AWC to check your revisions against student writing. One of the cardinal rules of creating or tweaking rubrics is to be sure they mirror what is actually in the writing.

- The AWC also provides attributes and language that may be useful as a starting point for teachers and students to invent their own rubrics, for instance, a task-specific rubric. Here is what Bay Area Writing Project leader Rebekah Caplan has to say about the value of creating rubrics:

> I believe students should have a hand in developing rubrics along with the teacher. As students read models of work in a genre, they should be building the "features" as they read more and more examples. (personal communication, April 21, 2016)

We agree with Caplan that building a rubric with students gives them both knowledge and authority. In the same vein, we have witnessed the potential of the AWC to give students—even those in second grade—jurisdiction over their writing and a deeper understanding of its qualities. We advise our readers to set a goal for their class as they get started with the AWC—one that might include a deeper understanding of what constitutes good writing.

WHAT TEACHERS HAVE TO SAY: PRINCIPLES FOR USING THE AWC

Teachers at the Central Texas Writing Project were among the many who re-invented the AWC for teaching writing in their own classrooms. Over a two-year period they worked together, asking questions, making sense of the descriptors, and putting the AWC to the test with students.

Early in their inquiry, these teachers found that using the AWC gave their students a common language for talking about writing and for thinking about how they might improve their writing. Each teacher worked independently to find the "best" way of using the AWC with her own students. As a group, they shared and adapted ideas and constructed a set of principles, presented in Figure 6.1, for using the AWC for instruction (Swain & LeMahieu, 2012, p. 63).

In 2008, the NWP conducted the Scoring Impact Study to find out the extent to which the AWC had value to teacher scorers. Initially, 325 teachers received the online survey. One hundred thirty-six (41.6%) responded. On a 6-point scale, 52% to 69% gave marks of 5 or 6, indicating that the assessment system gave them a deeper understanding of the characteristics of effective writing, of how to assess student writing, and of how to teach students to write (Swain & LeMahieu, 2012, p. 59).

In particular, teachers in the study commented on how their new understandings translated into classroom practice:

- I have a better/deeper understanding of the traits used in writing. This has helped me, guiding my mini-lessons, which has helped my students in their writing. (Swain et al., 2010, p. 18)

- I knew what to tell the students to look for as they started revising. (Swain et al., 2010, p. 22)
- I work with revision a lot more so that the scoring guide is a learning tool more than a summative evaluation. (Swain et al., 2010, p. 26)
- It has influenced the language I use when responding to student writing. This is so powerful! (Swain et al., 2010, p. 29)
- I involve the students in the process of evaluation more. Evaluating each other's and their own writing. (Swain et al., 2010, p. 31)

Clearly the statements cover a range of uses for the AWC, and they point to real pedagogical issues. Note especially the word *more*: More working with revision. More involving students in evaluation. More than a summative evaluation. The AWC opened the door for these teachers to do more of what's helpful for student writers. (And we hope to cut back on what isn't so useful.)

At the start of this book, we acknowledged that teachers need better tools for responding to and grading student writing. They need to know that when they spend time—*more* this or *more* that—their time translates into better student writing. More is not better unless it gets us results. So when the teachers who made the statements above said the AWC provided a guide for minilessons or language to jump-start the revision process, they were

Figure 6.1. Top Ten Principles for Using the Analytic Writing Continuum

1. Use LOTS of authentic dialogue. In order to make sense of the AWC and effective writing, students and teachers must talk with each other and other authors.

2. Teachers should model, demonstrate, and provide direct instruction for each AWC attribute and use high-quality literature to illustrate effective writing.

3. Students should identify each attribute by name and practice each attribute in their own writing.

4. AWC is a strength-based tool. It can help teachers identify where their students need to progress and it allows teachers to meet students where they are. It is the foundation of formative assessment as well as summative assessment.

5. The AWC should not be used as a rigid tool but as a flexible continuum. Make the AWC your own! Don't let it dictate your teaching or limit your students' writing.

6. Students should self-evaluate and self-assess in order to improve their writing.

7. Students and teachers should continuously look at their identity as writers and explore their strengths as developing writers.

8. Study and evaluate a piece of writing and not the writer.

9. Students and teachers need to be allowed to take risks.

10. Develop authentic writing and create opportunities for students to publish.

Source: Swain & LeMahieu, 2012, p. 63

talking about better ways to help students improve their writing, without necessarily more work. Perhaps even less.

MAKE THE ANALYTIC WRITING CONTINUUM YOUR OWN

We like to remember that the AWC journey started with inviting teachers to the table to provide the groundwork and the ground rules. Now the AWC has served as the system for scoring 48,475 papers nationally and has taken root in teacher professional development and in writing teachers' classrooms. Not often do assessing, teaching, and learning come together in this way. We encourage our colleagues to use whatever part of the Analytic Writing Continuum—large or small—in whatever way that will help students improve and take joy in their writing.

Afterword

When students, teachers, administrators, and policymakers select writing assessments, they seek out rubrics that feature precisely the right words aligned with state standards and superior technical qualities. They have hopes that the rubric itself will offer clear direction for both writers and writing. In *Assessing Writing, Teaching Writers: Putting the Analytic Writing Continuum to Work in Your Classroom*, Mary Ann Smith and Sherry Seale Swain compose a more complex and compelling writing assessment scene. They place the National Writing Project's Analytic Writing Continuum into conversation with the writing and its readers. Across multiple settings, they show how the AWC provides a common language in a dynamic system (see Figure A.1) that works toward improving writing and, ultimately, supporting writers so they can flourish.

Common language. As Smith and Swain illustrate, the AWC's carefully developed language *does* matter. In classroom after classroom, we see teachers and students using the AWC's language to establish a common frame of reference for what good writing looks like, how to "identify what works in a paper." Yet the AWC's language is not static. The development team recursively refined the language in response to both students' writing and the teachers who have scored writing. Teachers bringing the AWC into their classrooms sometimes simplified the language to meet their students where they are (e.g., Debbie Dehoney's second graders) and at other times worked with one or two attributes at a time to support students in developing their writing in one challenging area (e.g., Denise Mumm's eighth graders working on sentence fluency and diction).

The writing. While the AWC represents a crucial tool for building shared criteria, its language does not stand alone. Central to *Assessing Writing, Teaching Writers*, and to the AWC assessment system, is the students' writing. Indeed, the description of every score point for each attribute begins with the phrase "The writing." While the AWC's language ultimately can help students "see where they are on their own" (see Chapter 3 of this book), students' writing breathes life into the AWC's language. Emily Noble's vivid recounting of bringing students' writing into a professional devel-

Figure A.1. How the AWC Establishes a Common Frame of Reference

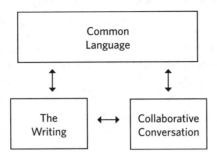

opment session illustrates how the language of the AWC scoring guide and the writing work together to help teachers see what next instructional steps can support students. As teachers and students work to improve writing and its teaching, the AWC and the writing literally and figuratively sit side-by-side on the table.

Collaborative conversation. Typical images of writing assessment conjure up a teacher sitting alone at her desk with a pile of papers or a vast, window-less ballroom with scores of teachers silently assigning numbers to paper after paper. While these static, silent images represent one dimension of writing assessment (including the AWC), what animates *Assessing Writing, Teaching Writers* and the AWC system is talk. In every story, Smith and Swain high-light conversations that foster collective meaning-making, the development of a shared vision, and even better writing and teaching. The stories provide windows into classrooms where, using the AWC's language, students bring questions about their writing to conferences with their teachers, during which they help each other improve. Through featuring these conversations, *Assessing Writing, Teaching Writers* demonstrates that the rubric and the writing serve as supporting tools in collaborative conversations.

Future directions for NWP's writing assessment work. Writing assessment continues to be an important component of the NWP's portfolio going forward. The foundational principles established through our decade-long work with the AWC guide our future work: creating attributes that NWP teachers, researchers, and programs value; focusing on the quality of the writing; addressing a range of writing, rather than a single task; developing scales sensitive enough to detect change over time; and building a system usable for teaching, learning, and research purposes. For example, we have developed the AWC for Source-Based Argument, which offers specific crite-ria for assessing writing in which putting evidence from external sources to work represents a key indicator of quality.

In addition, we are exploring how the affordances of technology can expand who can access NWP's writing assessment tools for classroom use, professional learning, and research purposes. As we employ these new tools, we are committed to maintaining the technical rigor of the system and working to achieve high rates of interrater agreement. We are equally committed to creating processes that facilitate conversations among teachers, between teachers and researchers, and between students and teachers about the qualities of writing. In this way, we will support new generations of teachers, and researchers as they continue to develop a shared vision of exemplary instruction of writing in every classroom in America.

—Linda Friedrich
Director of Research and Evaluation
National Writing Project

Technical Rigor and
Research on the System

Reliability. Table A.1 presents the operational reliabilities of scorers over eight years at NWP National Scoring Conferences. The interrater agreements (consensus among scorers) ranged from 88% to 91%, certainly adequate for the research that was the first purpose of the AWC Assessment System. These reliabilities suggest at least one attribute of the AWC—STANCE— proved more challenging for scorers to understand and apply to student papers. Over the years, the design team honed the definition of STANCE and NWP leaders created minilessons to use during the scorings.

Validity. Correlating scores from the AWC with other measures, notably state writing assessment systems, allows researchers to explore concurrent validity. Several local research teams have successfully included these analyses in their research designs. These analyses demonstrate appropriately high correlations and suggest that the AWC provides higher standards of performance and more useful information for instruction.

Utility of Use. A final area of ongoing inquiry monitors the AWC Assessment System in the interest of ensuring its utility to various users. Ongoing equating studies in which a large set of student papers is scored across years and settings ensure the comparability and consistency of standards. Newly initiated vertical equating studies in which sets of papers are scored at multiple grade levels monitor the interpretation of the standards at each level of the system and may interest those concerned with writing growth over time.

This information comes directly from *Assessment in a Culture of Inquiry: The Story of the National Writing Project's Analytic Writing Continuum* (Swain & LeMahieu, 2012, pp. 56 & 58) and from National Writing Project (2015) unpublished data on interrater reliability by attribute and year, available by contacting research@nwp.org.

Table A.1. National Writing Project Analytic Writing Continuum Reliabilities, 2005–2013

PERCENT AGREEMENT

Year (Convention)	Total Number of Papers	Double-Score Rate	Total	Content	Structure
2005–2013 Combined	48475	21%	90%	91%	91%

PERCENT AGREEMENT

Year (Convention)	Total Number of Papers	Stance	Sentence Fluency	Diction	Conventions
2005–2013 Combined	48475	88%	89%	91%	90%

Source. National Writing Project, Unpublished Data, 2015.

Notes

Chapter 1

1. Anne DiPardo, University of Colorado at Boulder; JoAnne Eresh, Achieve; Sandra Murphy, University of California, Davis; Gail Offen-Brown, University of California, Berkeley; Faye Peitzman, University of California, Los Angeles; Melanie Sperling, University of California, Riverside; Barbara Storms, California State University, East Bay; Paul LeMahieu, National Writing Project; Sherry Swain, National Writing Project.

Chapter 3

1. All Mathews quotes in this chapter are from Mathews, N. (2010). *Moving from summative to formative assessment: The move that makes rubrics a tool for teaching.* Unpublished manuscript.

2. All Dehoney quotes in this chapter are from Dehoney, D. (2010). *From reading into writing: AWC goes to the second grade.* Unpublished manuscript.

3. All Mumm quotes in this chapter are from Mumm, D. (2010). *Using the AWC to identify focus areas: Empowering student writers to revise.* Unpublished manuscript.

4. All Hetherington quotes in this chapter are from Hetherington, J. (2010). *A tale of task construal: How AWC changed my own and my students' perceptions of the task of writing.* Unpublished manuscript.

5. All Faile quotes in this chapter are from personal communication (June 19, 2009), unless otherwise noted.

Chapter 4

1. All Diedrich quotes in this chapter are from personal communication (July 19, 2013).

2. All Buchanan quotes in this chapter are from personal communication (September 19, 2013).

3. All Noble quotes in this chapter are from personal communication (September 19, 2013).

4. All Sheerman quotes in this chapter are from personal communication (July 11, 2016).

Chapter 6

1. All Diedrich quotes in this chapter are from personal communication (April 23, 2016).

References

Alber, R. (2012, February 6). Do you write with your students? *Edutopia*. Retrieved from www.edutopia.org/blog/writing-students-literacy-rebecca-alber.

Britton, J. (1972). *Language and learning*. Middlesex, England: Penguin Books.

Brookhart, S. (2013). *How to create and use rubrics for formative assessment and grading*. Alexandria, VA: Association for Supervision and Curriculum Development. Retrieved from www.ascd.org/publications/books/112001/chapters/What-Are-Rubrics-and-Why-Are-They-Important%C2%A2.aspx

Brooks, D. (2013, December 30). The Sidney Awards, Part 2. *New York Times*. Retrieved from http://www.nytimes.com/2013/12/31/opinion/brooks-the-sidney-awards-part-2.html?_r=0

Chiseri-Strater, E., & Sunstein, B. (2006). *What works: A practical guide for teacher research*. Portsmouth, NH: Heinemann.

Christensen, L. (2003). The politics of correction: How we can nurture students in their writing. *The Quarterly, 25*(4). Retrieved from www.nwp.org/cs/public/print/resource/951

Council of Chief State School Officers (CCSSO) & the National Governors Association (NGA). (2010). *Common core state standards for English language arts and literacy in history/social studies, science, and technical subjects*. Washington, DC: National Governors Association. Retrieved from *Common Core State Standards Initiative* website at www.corestandards.org/the-standards

Council of Chief State School Officers (CCSSO) & the National Governors Association (NGA). (2016). *Common core state standards initiative. English language arts standards: Students who are college and career ready in reading, writing, speaking, listening, & language*. Retrieved from www.corestandards.org/ELA-Literacy/introduction/students-who-are-college-and-career-ready-in-reading-writing-speaking-listening-language/

Davies, A., & LeMahieu, P. (2003). Assessment for learning: Reconsidering portfolios and research evidence. In M. Segers, F. Dochy, & E. Cacallar (Eds.), *Optimising new modes of assessment: In search of qualities and standards* (pp. 141–169). Dordecht, The Netherlands: Kluwer Academic Publishers.

Dehoney, D. (2010). *From reading into writing: AWC goes to the second grade*. Unpublished manuscript.

Dehoney, F. (2010). *How this all came to be*. Unpublished manuscript.

Devlin, R. (2003). Jeff Wilhelm: You gotta BE a teacher-researcher. *The Voice, 8*(1). Retrieved from www.nwp.org/cs/public/print/resource/510

Diedrich, P. (2010). *Constructive chaos: Differentiating evaluation because inflexible rubrics fit few*. Unpublished manuscript.

DiPardo, A., Storms, B. A., & Selland, M. (2011). Seeing voices: Assessing writerly stance in the NWP Analytic Writing Continuum. *Assessing Writing, 16*(3), 170–188.

Dorfman, L., & Cappeli, R. (2007). *Mentor texts: Teaching writing through children's literature, K–6.* Portland, ME: Stenhouse.

Elbow, P. (1999). *Everyone can write: Essays toward a hopeful theory of writing and teaching writing.* New York, NY: Oxford University Press.

Freedland, J. (2013, November 19). The selfie's screaming narcissism masks an urge to connect. *The Guardian.* Retrieved from www.theguardian.com/commentisfree/2013/nov/19/selfie-narcissism-oxford-dictionary-word

Friedrich, L., Simons, E. R., & Tateishi, C. (2005). Building inquiry communities and leadership for equity. In L. Friedrich, T. Malarkey, E. R. Simons, C. Tateishi, & M. Williams (Eds.), *Working toward equity: Writings and resources from the teacher research collaborative* (pp. 125–128). Berkeley, CA: National Writing Project.

Gallagher, K. (2011). *Write like this: Teaching real-world writing through modeling and mentor texts.* Portland, ME: Stenhouse.

Goswami, D., Lewis, C., Rutherford, M., & Waff, D. (2009). *On teacher inquiry: Approaches to language and literacy research.* New York, NY: Teachers College Press.

Graham, S., Harris, K., & Hebert, M. A. (2011). *Informing writing: The benefits of formative assessment.* A Carnegie Corporation Time to Act report. Washington, DC: Alliance for Excellent Education.

Graham, S. & Harris, K. (2013). Designing an effective writing program. In S. Graham, C.A. MacArthur, & J. Fitzgerald (Eds.), *Best practices in writing instruction* (2nd ed., pp. 3–25). New York, NY: Guilford Press.

Graham, S., & Perin, D. (2007). *Writing next: Effective strategies to improve writing of adolescents in middle and high schools.* A report to Carnegie Corporation of New York. New York, NY: Carnegie Corporation.

Gray, J. (2000). *Teachers at the center: A memoir of the early years of the National Writing Project.* Berkeley, CA: National Writing Project.

Hetherington, J. (2010). *A tale of task construal: How AWC changed my own and my students' perceptions of the task of writing.* Unpublished manuscript.

Hillocks, G. (2002). *The testing trap: How state writing assessments control learning.* New York, NY: Teachers College Press.

Hillocks, G., Jr. (1986). *Research on written composition: New directions for teaching.* Paper presented at the National Conference on Research in English/ERIC Clearinghouse on Reading and Communication Skills, Urbana, IL.

Hultman, Connor. (2015, May 9). *Baby blue shack for Rural Voices Radio.* Jackson, MS: Mississippi Public Broadcasting, Mississippi State University, Mississippi Writing/Thinking Institute. Retrieved from www.themsms.org/rural-voices-radio/

Koch, R. (2004). Where writing really begins. *The Quarterly, 26*(4). Retrieved from www.nwp.org/cs/public/print/resource/2143

MacArthur, C. (2016). Instruction in evaluation and revision. In C. MacArthur, S. Graham, & J. Fitzgerald (Eds.), *Handbook of writing research* (2nd ed.). New York, NY: The Guilford Press.

Mathews, N. (2010). *Moving from summative to formative assessment: The move that makes rubrics a tool for teaching.* Unpublished manuscript.

Mohr, M., Rogers, C., Sanford, B., Nocerino, M.A., MacLean, M., & Clawson, S. (2003). *Teacher research for better schools.* New York, NY: Teachers College Press.

Mumm, D. (2010). *Using the AWC to identify focus areas: Empowering student writers to revise.* Unpublished manuscript.

Murphy, S., & Smith, M.A. (in press). The faraway stick cannot kill the nearby snake. In C. Bazerman (Ed.), *The lifespan development of writing.* Urbana, IL: National Council of Teachers of English.

Murphy, S., & Smith, M. A. (2015). *Uncommonly good ideas: Teaching writing in the Common Core era.* New York, NY: Teachers College Press.

National Writing Project. (2015). *Inter-rater reliabilities by attribute and year.* Unpublished data. Available by contacting research@nwp.org.

Northwest Regional Educational Laboratory. (2005). *Trait definition.* Retrieved from http://educationnorthwest.org/traits/trait-definitions (Accessed March 2013).

NWP Research and Evaluation Unit. (2010, July). *Writing project professional development continues to yield gains in student writing achievement* (Research Brief No. 2). Berkeley CA: National Writing Project. Retrieved from www.nwp.org/cs/public/download/nwp_file/14004/FINAL_2010_Research_Brief.pdf?x-r=pcfile_d

O'Donnell-Allen, C. (2012, September 26). The best writing teachers are writers themselves. *The Atlantic.* Retrieved from www.theatlantic.com/national/archive/2012/09/the-best-writing-teachers-are-writers-themselves/262858/

Olson, C. B., Scarcella, R., & Matuchniak, T. (2015). *Helping English learners to write: Meeting common core standards, grades 6–12.* New York, NY: Teachers College Press.

Peterson, A. (1996). *The writer's workout book: 113 stretches toward better prose.* Berkeley, CA: National Writing Project.

Smith, M.A. (2003). Learning about ourselves from looking at others. *The Quarterly, 25*(1). Retrieved from www.nwp.org/cs/public/print/resource/528

Spandel, V. (2005). *The 9 rights of every writer: A guide for teachers.* Portsmouth, NH: Heinemann.

Spandel, V., & Stiggins, R. (1997). *Creating writers: Linking writing assessment and instruction* (2nd ed.). White Plains, NY: Longman.

Sperling, M., & Appleman, D. (2011). Voice in the context of literacy studies. *Reading Research Quarterly, 46*(1), 70–84.

Swain, S. S., Graves, R. L., & Morse, D. T. (2010). The final free modifier, once more. *English Journal, 99*(4), 84–89.

Swain, S. S., Graves, R. L., & Morse, D. T. (2015). The emerging shape of voice. *English Journal, 104*(5), 30–36.

Swain, S. S., & LeMahieu, P. (2012). Assessment in a culture of inquiry: The story of the National Writing Project's Analytic Writing Continuum. In N. Elliot & L. Perelman (Eds.), *Writing assessment in the 21st century: Essays in honor of Edward M. White* (pp. 45–66). Cresskill, NJ: Hampton Press.

Swain, S. S., LeMahieu, P., Sperling, M., Murphy, S., Fessehaie, S., & Smith, M. A. (2010). *The impact of the National Writing Project scoring conferences.* Paper presented at the meeting of Writing Research Across Borders II (February 17–20), George Mason University.

Tierney, J. (2013, January 9). Why teachers secretly hate grading papers. *The Atlantic.* Retrieved from www.theatlantic.com/national/archive/2013/01/why-teachers-secretly-hate-grading-papers/266931/

Troia, G. (2013). Writing instruction within a response-to-intervention framework. In S. Graham, C. A. MacArthur, & J. Fitzgerald (Eds.), *Best practices in writing instruction* (2nd ed.) (pp. 403–427). New York: NY: Guilford Press.

White, E. (2007). *Assigning, responding, evaluating: A writing teacher's guide* (4th ed.). New York, NY: Bedford/St. Martin's.

Williamson, M. (1993). An introduction to holistic scoring. In M. M. Williamson & B. Huot (Eds.), *Validating holistic scoring for writing assessment: Theoretical and empirical foundations* (pp. 45–78). Cresskill, NJ: Hampton Press, Inc.

Index

About the Authors

Mary Ann Smith directed the Bay Area and California Writing Projects and served as Director of Government Relations and Public Affairs for the National Writing Project. A former secondary teacher, she has written many articles and books about teaching and assessing writing, including *Uncommonly Good Ideas: Teaching Writing in the Common Core Era* with Sandra Murphy.

Sherry Seale Swain directed the Mississippi Writing/Thinking Institute at Mississippi State University before becoming Senior Research Associate for the National Writing Project. A former primary teacher, she has written widely about teaching and assessing writing. Currently, she also is the director and producer of Mississippi Rural Voices Radio.